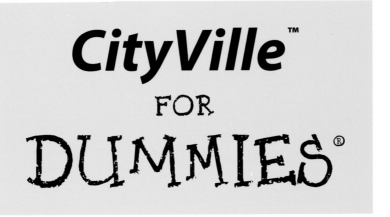

CityVille™
FOR
DUMMIES®

by Kyle Orland and Michelle Oxman

WILEY

Wiley Publishing, Inc.

CityVille™ For Dummies®

Published by
Wiley Publishing, Inc.
111 River Street
Hoboken, NJ 07030-5774
www.wiley.com

Copyright © 2011 by Wiley Publishing, Inc., Indianapolis, Indiana

Published by Wiley Publishing, Inc., Indianapolis, Indiana

Published simultaneously in Canada

For general information on our other products and services, please contact our Customer Care Department within the U.S. at 877-762-2974, outside the U.S. at 317-572-3993, or fax 317-572-4002.

For technical support, please visit www.wiley.com/techsupport.

Wiley also publishes its books in a variety of electronic formats and by print-on-demand. Not all content that is available in standard print versions of this book may appear or be packaged in all book formats. If you have purchased a version of this book that did not include media that is referenced by or accompanies a standard print version, you may request this media by visiting http://booksupport.wiley.com. For more information about Wiley products, visit us at www.wiley.com.

Library of Congress Control Number is available from the publisher.

ISBN: 978-1-118-08337-6

Manufactured in the United States of America

10 9 8 7 6 5 4 3 2 1

WILEY

About the Authors

Kyle Orland (http://www.kyleorland.com) has been writing about videogames in one form or another since 1997, when he started fan site Super Mario Bros. HQ (http://www.smbhq.com) at the tender age of 14. Since then, he's become a full-time videogame expert and freelancer, with work appearing in *Electronic Gaming Monthly*, *Paste Magazine*, NPR, Gamespot, Joystiq, and The Escapist, among many other outlets.

Currently, Kyle acts as a Contributing News Editor for premiere game development community Gamasutra.com. He's been quoted as a videogame expert in *The New York Times*, *The Washington Post*, NPR, G4 TV and TheStreet.com, among others.

This is Kyle's third Dummies book, after *Wii For Dummies* and *FarmVille For Dummies*, co-authored by Angela Morales. He's also the co-author of *The Videogame Style Guide and Reference Manual* (http://www.gamestyleguide.com), the first ever guide to usage and style focused on the gaming realm.

Kyle's favorite game of all time is *Super Mario 64*.

Michelle Krasniak Oxman is a writer and consultant living in Minneapolis, MN. She owns her own copywriting business where she creates website content, blog articles and profile interviews for clients all over the world. She has been writing professionally for the past decade and her journalism training and technical writing experience has served her well when it comes to creating content for companies in a variety of industries. In addition to writing, Michelle has served as Technical Editor for a number of social media-related "Dummies" books and she recently returned to school to get her Master of Business Communication degree. A lover of everything social media, Michelle likes to spend her free time connecting with others through social gaming.

Dedication

To my wife Michelle, who never let's me believe there's anything I can't do.

Kyle Orland

To my husband Jeff, thank you for putting up with me when my attention was more on my City than it was on you. Your words of encouragement have always kept me going and you are my perfect partner in crime. I love you!

Thank you to my family for all of the love, support and encouragement you have given me throughout the years. I am who I am because of you.

To all of my friends who are scattered around the country. Though we may not see each other frequently or talk often, I hold a warm spot in my heart for each of you.

Finally, to my faithful bulldog Simon, I ignored you for many hours while writing this. I promise to spoil you even more to make up for it.

Michelle Oxman

Authors' Acknowledgments

Thanks to my wife Michelle for tolerating all the late nights I spent chained to my desk meeting deadlines, and for not minding too much when I woke her up trying to sneak back into bed much too late. Thanks again to A. Mike for helping set up my sweet dual-monitor desktop set up that made editing text and playing the game at the same time quite easy.

Thanks to Libe Goad, who gave me a shot at AOL's Games.com — The Blog and got me into this whole social gaming thing in the first place. Thanks to Pat O'Brien, Amy Fandrei, and all the other people at Wiley who saw our prose through to polished completion. Thanks to Jason Schreier for losing his soul to our tech editing needs.

Thanks to Zynga for making a product that gets millions more people to realize that video games aren't just for teenage boys and social recluses. Thanks to Google for making the Chrome browser, which I used for all the web-related things in this book and was quite pleased with. Finally, thanks to 9gag.com for providing welcome distraction when I felt I just couldn't write another word about decoration placement.

Kyle Orland

I'd like to thank Acquisitions Editor Amy Fandrei for getting me on the "other side" of a Dummies book this time around. I really appreciate the opportunity! Thanks to our Project Editor Pat O'Brien and the rest of the Dummies editorial team for all of the hard work they put in behind the scenes to make Dummies books the fantastic resources they are.

A special thank you to my sister Sarah Krasniak and my good friend Danielle Charpentier for being "on-call" when I needed some neighborly help in CityVille. You ladies are the epitome of what it means to be a good neighbor. Thank you to my co-author Kyle Orland for all of your help. You taught me a lot about the Dummies writing process.

I never would have been able to write this book if it weren't for the help of all of my CityVille neighbors from around the world. While we may not have met in person, you all pitched in to lend a helping hand whenever I needed it.

Finally, thank you to Zynga tech support for patiently answering any questions I had. You're one of the best customer support teams out there. Keep up the good work!

Michelle Oxman

Publisher's Acknowledgments

We're proud of this book; please send us your comments at http://dummies.custhelp.com. For other comments, please contact our Customer Care Department within the U.S. at 877-762-2974, outside the U.S. at 317-572-3993, or fax 317-572-4002.

Some of the people who helped bring this book to market include the following:

Acquisitions, Editorial, and Media Development

Project Editor: Pat O'Brien

Acquisitions Editor: Amy Fandrei

Copy Editor: Jennifer Riggs

Technical Editor: Jason Schreier

Editorial Manager: Kevin Kirschner

Media Development Project Manager: Laura Moss-Hollister

Media Development Assistant Project Manager: Jenny Swisher

Media Development Associate Producers: Josh Frank, Marilyn Hummel, Douglas Kuhn, and Shawn Patrick

Editorial Assistant: Amanda Graham

Sr. Editorial Assistant: Cherie Case

Cartoons: Rich Tennant (www.the5thwave.com)

Composition Services

Project Coordinator: Patrick Redmond

Layout and Graphics: Joyce Haughey, Corrie Socolovitch

Proofreader: ConText Editorial Services, Inc.

Indexer: Valerie Haynes Perry

Publishing and Editorial for Technology Dummies

Richard Swadley, Vice President and Executive Group Publisher

Andy Cummings, Vice President and Publisher

Mary Bednarek, Executive Acquisitions Director

Mary C. Corder, Editorial Director

Publishing for Consumer Dummies

Diane Graves Steele, Vice President and Publisher

Composition Services

Debbie Stailey, Director of Composition Services

Contents at a Glance

Table of Contents

Introduction

*I*f you're reading this book, chances are you're interested in playing *CityVille,* the largest social game ever made. You may have heard about it from your friend or stumbled across it after signing up for a Facebook account. Either way, CityVille has attracted more than 90 million active users and from the looks of it, will also be recruiting you to join its solid fan base of dedicated players.

Welcome to the wonderful world of CityVille, a world of urban bliss where there's no pollution, no crime, and no taxes. Get ready to flex your city planning muscles and set up the town of your dreams.

As you read this book and figure out how to play CityVille, we hope you'll have some fun along the way as we provide you with everything you need to know to begin your alternate life as an Internet tycoon.

About This Book

Congrats! You bought a *For Dummies* book so you can find out more about CityVille and how to play it. This book is designed to help you jump-start your life as a virtual city manager. We wrote it with the *novice* player in mind — someone who has never played CityVille or a social game in general. Because playing CityVille requires that you have a Facebook account, we also walk you through the steps of setting one up.

You don't need to be a computer nerd or a skilled gamer to use this book, but we do assume that you have an Internet connection and a passing familiarity with how to use a computer and a Web browser. Beyond that, we've compiled everything you need to know about playing CityVille in this printed edition, which takes you through each part of the city building process step by step. There's no need to become a hardcore gamer to enjoy CityVille — the game is meant to be an enjoyable experience that anyone can master, even you!

Sometimes, the best way to get better at something is by doing, and CityVille is no different. Don't be afraid to try things and click around your city to see what different things do. Remember, you have this nifty guide as a resource to help you cross any technology gap you may be facing and overcome any fear of the unknown that virtual city management entails.

Note: All the information in this book was accurate to the best of our knowledge at the time of publication. CityVille is in a constant state of change. There are likely to be changes and new content introduced to CityVille in the future that will not be addressed by this book. (We know a lot about CityVille, but we're not psychic, after all.) However, what we have written about the fundamentals of city building should not change significantly, and will remain useful for you as a reader well into the future.

Conventions Used in This Book

In this book, we use numbered steps, bullet lists, and pictures for your reference. You also find a few sidebars that contain information that isn't considered required reading, but may help you understand a topic a little better. Web addresses appear in a special monotype font that looks like this: www.dummies.com.

This book measures in-game items like buildings and decorations in terms of *blocks.* The CityVille play area is made up of a regular grid of these square blocks, which you can see as a faint green outline when you place most items. If a building is said to be 6 x 3 in size, for instance, that means it takes up the length of 6 blocks on one edge and the length of 3 blocks along the other edge, or an area of 18 total square blocks.

How This Book Is Organized

CityVille For Dummies consists of six parts. Of course we hope you read this book with eagerness from cover to cover, but if you'd rather use it as a reference for specific situations as they arise, that's okay, too. We refer you to other chapters when appropriate if you need information that's found elsewhere in the book, so don't worry about missing something if you skip around.

Part 1: Basic City Living

This first part introduces you to CityVille, including what the game is, how it fits into the social-gaming genre, and why so many people play it. You find out how to set up a Facebook account and a CityVille account, as well as how to navigate your way through CityVille menus. We also walk you through other basics, such as setting up your first city and adding neighbors.

Part II: Seeking Your CityVille Fortune

Part II is all about building your city into a resource-making powerhouse. We discuss the various resources you can collect in the game — including Coins, Cash, Goods, and Energy — and how to structure your city to earn them as quickly and efficiently as possible. We also take you through the game's quest system, walking your through the path to mayorship and beyond.

Part III: Staying Safe and Up to Date on CityVille

The Internet can be a scary thing for many people, but don't worry; we have you covered. In this part, we discuss some ways that you can play CityVille more safely and make yourself a more informed user. We also let you in on how to contact *Zynga,* the game's developer, and provide you with a few Web resources to help you get your farming fix, after you finish reading this book that is.

Part IV: The Part of Tens

What would a *For Dummies* book be without the Part of Tens section of top ten lists? Our top tens include a list of different types of cities, a list of the most-wanted items, and finally a go-to list of general tips to keep in mind when building your city.

Icons Used in This Book

We use various icons in the margins of this book to point out specific information that you may find useful. We use the following icons:

This icon calls attention to any tip or trick that you can use to enhance your game play.

This icon emphasizes points that you should attempt to retain. If you remember these special points, you'll be a better player.

If you see this icon, read it! Warnings can prevent you from making a big mistake that could be hazardous to your city (or computer).

This is the geeky stuff that you can safely skip. However, we felt it deserved a place in the, book so you may be interested in reading it.

Where to Go from Here

The world of CityVille awaits you! You no doubt have a lot of questions, but don't worry, that's a good thing. Take a look at the Table of Contents, flip through the pages, and see whether anything sparks your interest. If you know nothing about CityVille, you may want to start at the beginning with Chapter 1.

If you have specific questions or comments about this book, or maybe a lingering question we didn't address, you can contact Michelle at mishikraz@gmail.com or Kyle at kyle.orland@gmail.com.

Thank you for buying our book, and we sincerely hope that it is helpful to you as a CityVille player.

Part I
Basic City Living

*1*n this part, we introduce you to the phenomenon called CityVille, the web-based game that has captured the attention of millions of people around the world in just a few short months.

Chapter 1 talks about why people enjoy playing CityVille and gives you a general overview on what the game is all about.

Find out what you have to do in order to get started playing the game including the computing power you need and setting up a Facebook account in Chapter 2.

In Chapter 3, find out about the different menus in CityVille that are the key to navigating around your City.

Learn about the Build menu and all of the items available for purchase in Chapter 4.

Chapter 5 gets you off on the right foot by taking you through creating your first City, step-by-step.

Learn the importance of finding the right neighbors and how it's a two-way street when it comes to lending and accepting help from them in Chapter 6.

Welcome to CityVille

In This Chapter

▷ Understanding why people play CityVille

▷ Getting a grasp of the key CityVille concepts

*C*ityVille is a Web-based city life simulation game produced by *Zynga,* a gaming company. In contrast to many computer games that you have to buy on a disc, anyone with an Internet connection and a Facebook account can load CityVille in his Web browser and play for free in an instant. The ease of access is one of the reasons CityVille has become so popular.

The basic concept of CityVille is relatively simple. You manage your virtual city by constructing buildings, such as stores, homes, and community buildings, planting crops to harvest Goods to supply your stores, and collecting rent on your dwellings. By completing these tasks, you earn Coins that you can spend to expand and upgrade your city. You also gain Experience Points, which go toward earning new levels, new items, and new game play opportunities in your city. Through weeks and months of dedicated work in your city, you can build your initial small, empty city into a massive, thriving mega-city bustling with life.

Whereas most games cease to exist when you turn them off, crops in your city continue to grow, businesses continue to sell Goods, and homeowners continue to pay rent, even when you're not actively playing. Fully grown crops can wither on the vine if they're not harvested promptly, and Goods on your ships can spoil in the same way. Therefore, you may have to plan your daily schedule around your CityVille play time to some extent. This time-sensitive game play can be a little annoying, but the game doesn't require a heavy time investment — just a half hour to an hour each day is enough to keep up with most basic tasks. Of course, you can play much more than that. The sheer time-sucking amount of stuff to do and collect in your city helps make CityVille one of the most addictive games out there as more than 100 million users, as of this writing, can attest.

This chapter tells you what CityVille is and the basics of playing the game. We also provide some tips to help you avoid getting too engrossed in the magical world of being a virtual Mayor of your own city. Welcome to a thriving metropolis and city life — all controlled with the click of your mouse.

Why Millions Play CityVille (and You Should, Too!)

Surely some common factor must make CityVille appealing to so many millions. Maybe deep down inside, everyone wants to be the Mayor of their own city. Perhaps people are intrigued by the idea that they're responsible for creating a thriving metropolis.

Whatever the case, CityVille attracts people from all walks of life. The virtual Mayors of CityVille represent a broad range of backgrounds and professions. Business professionals, stay-at-home moms, doctors, the unemployed, stockbrokers, technology gurus, college students, and retirees live second lives as diligent Internet city slickers. Even if you don't play, chances are good that you know somebody who enjoys virtual city life.

Ease of play

Satisfying game play sessions in CityVille can last as little as a few minutes, and real-world interruptions don't ruin your progress because the game saves your progress constantly. What's more, playing CityVille doesn't require your full attention. You can easily play the game while multitasking on a conference call, watching a mindless TV show, or waiting for dinner to cook.

With a laptop, CityVille can even help fill those wasted wait times that can seem to fill up a day. Whether a lull in your work schedule, an otherwise boring airport layover, a long delay in a doctor's waiting room, or a ride on the subway, you can make it more tolerable by cashing in on Coins from the day's business sales and rent collections.

Aside from occasional withered crops and spoiled Goods, CityVille has few of the frustrating setbacks that can sour the experience of traditional games, such as impassably tough challenges, frustratingly obtuse puzzles, or Game Over screens. Additionally, in contrast to some games that require hours of focused attention just to get up to speed, CityVille is designed to be easy to grasp almost immediately. Of course, every game has experts who make it to higher levels than others, and CityVille is no different, but anyone — including you! — can become a veteran if you just keep playing.

The challenge of self-improvement and competition

How do you beat CityVille? Easy answer: You don't. Rather than display a final challenge and a Congratulations, You Win! screen signaling the end of the game, CityVille features a never-ending cycle of city tasks and quests just for the sake of having them.

That doesn't mean the game doesn't have any goals, though. The possibilities for self-improvement are nearly endless, depending on what aspects of the game are most important to you. You can

- ✐ Gain Experience Points and reach higher levels quickly. There are currently 80 levels.
- ✐ Amass as many items as possible.
- ✐ Focus on growing and mastering all possible businesses.
- ✐ Amass a fortune in City Coins.
- ✐ Earn every possible collection.

What you do with your CityVille experience is largely up to you. Improving your statistics for your own sake is all well and good, but many Mayors also turn CityVille into a competition with their friends, battling to reach ever-higher accomplishments before their neighbors do. Keeping up with the Joneses applies just as much in the virtual realm as the real world, and many CityVille players take beating their neighbors to that next goal incredibly seriously.

Creativity

The virtual world of CityVille isn't just a place to live out your city life fantasies; it can also be a canvas to express your artistic sensibilities. By carefully setting down items in specific arrangements, you can create anything from re-creations of famous paintings and cartoon characters to CityVille-ized versions of real-world architecture and three-dimensional visual effects. True, these creations don't serve any larger economic purpose in your city, but as any artist can tell you, sometimes creation is its own reward.

One of the most common methods for creating beautiful cities is by placing plots of flowers, trees, and Arboretums in open places around businesses and dwellings. With each decoration costing 50 to 60,000 City Coins (see Chapter 7 for more about amassing City Coins), the costs can add up quickly, but it's one action that can generate beautiful results, as shown in Figure 1-1. An added bonus? For each decoration you place around a dwelling or business, it increases the payout of that building by a certain percentage that depends on the specific decoration. Talk about killing two birds with one stone!

Figure 1-1: Beautiful gardens made using CityVille flower arrangements.

Entertainment and escape

Of course, the primary purpose of any game is entertainment, and CityVille is no different. Most virtual Mayors would probably cite entertainment or escape as the main reason they love playing CityVille, and in today's fast-paced world, who can blame them? For many people, escaping to the virtual world of CityVille is the next best thing to a real vacation that may be impossible for any number of reasons. The game provides an easy, cheap way to relieve stress, relax, and unwind. There's something about the familiar rhythm of the building and collection cycle that helps make the stresses of everyday life seem just a little less stressful. The camaraderie and companionship generated by interacting with CityVille neighbors can also provide a sense of community.

Social gaming and CityVille

Although CityVille can technically be played as a single-player game, it takes advantage of Facebook's social networking framework to encourage interaction with other players.

Socializing with other players by visiting their cities, sharing gifts, and helping them perform work in their cities are key to getting the most out of the game. This focus on social interaction puts CityVille at the forefront of the new social gaming trend. Simply defined, a *social game* is any game with social interaction.

Although social gaming isn't an entirely new concept, it has recently become one of the hottest sectors of the video game industry. Because of the success of games, such as CityVille and FarmVille, many game developers are eager to get a piece of the social gaming pie.

And that pie isn't small by any means. Whereas tens of millions of people play traditional video games on consoles and personal computers, simple social games have attracted *hundreds* of millions of players, many of whom never bothered to keep up with the competitive, reflex-heavy, and technically complex world of traditional video games.

Understanding the Key Concepts of CityVille

Throughout this book, we cover the various facets of CityVille in great detail, of course, but the following sections give you the basics of how CityVille works and what you actually do in the game.

You get your own city

After you install the CityVille app on your Facebook account (see how in Chapter 2), you start with a small, mostly empty city, which we call the *play area*. This city, and the game itself, aren't actually stored permanently on your computer, but instead they are hosted on the CityVille servers maintained by Zynga.

Your virtual city slicker begins the game owning a few plots of plowed land with strawberries pre-planted, and a bit of money, denominated in CityVille's two in-game currencies: City Cash and City Coins (which we discuss in detail in Chapter 7). You can purchase more currency using real money, but you can also earn it simply by playing the game (see the next section).

Customizing and growing your city to your desired specifications forms the bulk of the game. To start, however, you're set up with one house, a barn for Goods storage, some farming plots with strawberries, and an empty plot for a neighbor to open a franchise store.

Don't be worried about getting the hang of the game, though. Right from the beginning, you have the helpful guide Samantha who walks you through the ins and outs of building up your city.

You place houses, businesses, crops, and decorations

That little bit of money you start with won't last very long if you don't invest it in profitable items. Using the mouse, you click around your city using in-game tools (as we discuss in Chapter 3) to plow plots of land, plant crops, and, eventually, harvest those crops for goods and collectable items, which are discussed more in Chapter 7. Another good idea is to build another house or two as a way to earn some rent and build a business to bring in more revenue. All these items can be found in the Build menu that we discuss in more detail in Chapter 4.

Crops grow, ripen, and eventually wither when you're not actively playing the game. You have to check and harvest them on a real-time schedule. The same thing happens when you start using piers to bring in shipments of Goods from faraway lands, which we discuss more in Chapter 4. You can also purchase things, such as sidewalks trees, animals, flowers, and statues, that increase the payout of your buildings when they're nearby. All these items mean one thing — more City Coins in your virtual pocket!

You collect rent and Goods

CityVille currency isn't just good for generating more currency through building homes to collect rent or business to collect profits; it's also good for buying decorations that make your city uniquely yours.

Think of decorating as a virtual, city-themed doll house, with a selection of accessories waiting to fill it up.

The best part about placing decorations is that when they're placed around dwellings or businesses, most of them increase the payout for that building by a certain percentage. For the ones that increase the building's payout, the percentages range from 1 percent all the way up to a whopping 64 percent! We discuss utilizing decorations to increase revenue more in Chapters 4 and 9.

You help your neighbors (and they help you)

As a social game, CityVille is partially focused on helping fellow players, or *neighbors*. CityVille neighbors are a subset of your Facebook friends, so you have to be friends with a person on Facebook in order to be CityVille neighbors. Obviously not all of your Facebook friends play CityVille, though. But wouldn't it be great if they did?

Avoiding CityVille "addiction"

If you find that you neglect aspects of your daily life, such as showering, eating, taking care of your pets or kids, or even going to work, to play CityVille, you may be addicted! It's very important that you maintain limits when logging on and taking on the role of Mayor of your virtual city. When other, more important aspects of your day-to-day life suffer because of your game playing, take a step back and get back to the real world.

Certainly there are many worse things to be addicted to than video games, but getting a bit too engrossed in the virtual world is a very real risk for some people. CityVille players can be especially susceptible to the effects of addiction for several reasons. The game's time-sensitive crops encourage players to check in frequently to avoid withering. A built-in community of fellow players can draw people away from their friends and family in the real world. Weekly updates and limited-edition items keep players coming back to see what's coming next. Random gifts and hidden items have a slot-machine–like effect on some players, keeping them clicking for that next random reward.

If you ever get to the point where you start thinking, "I can't stop watching my crops!" or "I have to make sure all my businesses make money constantly!" you're not alone. Many people engage in virtual city life not just for an occasional escape but also as a constant way to avoid real-world problems and responsibilities. Addiction can happen to anyone.

Don't let the risk of addiction threaten to ruin the fun you can have building your virtual city. Instead, follow these tips for avoiding addiction — not just in CityVille, but with any video or computer game:

- **Limit the time you spend playing.** Set a strict time limit for how much you allow yourself to play each day — a half hour or an hour, perhaps — and stick to it religiously. Use a stopwatch or a kitchen timer to help remind yourself to stop playing when your time is up.

- **Schedule your game play.** Set aside a specific time every day to play the game, and don't let yourself log in before or after that time. Use the scheduled play time as something to look forward to throughout the day rather than allow the game to kill productive time.

- **Make a list of your real-world obligations for the day.** Reward yourself with a quick visit to CityVille after you complete everything on your list — but not before.

- **Plant crops that fit your lifestyle.** Crops that sprout every four hours demand constant attention and frequent logins to harvest. Planting crops with longer growing times requires less frequent play time to get them harvested; it also gives you a longer margin of error for avoiding withered crops.

- **Utilize dwellings and buildings with longer collection cycles.** Just like crops, buildings in CityVille have collection cycles that vary. Choose buildings with longer collection cycles, such as a day or two, and businesses that require a higher number of Goods so they don't run out as quickly. For more information on choosing the right combination of buildings to fit your needs, see Chapter 9.

You can help your neighbors by sending them free gifts or by visiting their cities and performing some basic tasks daily. After you've been playing for a while and have amassed enough neighbors, you can open franchise stores in their cities as well as unlock some fun new things, such as decorations and buildings, in the Build menu. Of course, your neighbors can do all these things for you as well, forming a big, reciprocal cycle of goodwill.

It's not all sunshine and happiness, though — some players can get pretty competitive about CityVille, working hard to make their cities that much more spectacular than those of their neighbors. Chapter 6 discusses interacting with neighbors in much more detail.

You complete goals and upgrade your city

As you perform various actions and buy various in-game items in CityVille, you earn *Experience Points* (XP) to denote your progress. Earning enough Experience Points grants you a new *level,* which often comes with the ability to buy new items (see Chapter 7).

As you *level up,* as the process of earning new levels is known, you can purchase important upgrade items, such as storage buildings and city expansions (see Chapter 4), to help your city hold even more items.

Besides Experience Points and levels, you can also earn more specific *achievements,* or *quests,* for successfully completing in-game goals. These quests, which we discuss in Chapter 8, start the minute you open your city for business and continue throughout the game. They can be as simple as planting and harvesting a certain crop to completing a collection (see Chapter 7) to cash it in for a particular item.

Goals are fun little challenges you're presented with throughout the game, and successfully completing the goals will eventually lead you to become the Mayor of your city and eventually Governor!

This continuous process of building and maintaining your city has no end point. Zynga constantly adds new features and new items to keep long-time players interested. Players also often change which aspect of the game and which goals they want to focus on as they continue to play (see Chapter 8).

2

Getting Set Up to Play

In This Chapter

▶ Getting what you need to get started with CityVille

▶ Creating a Facebook account

▶ Installing, bookmarking, and getting neighbors in CityVille

▶ Staying involved with CityVille on Facebook, Twitter, and forums

So you're ready to become a virtual mayor, eh? Well, we're happy to help you do that, but first things first: You have to make sure you have what you need to get started. Using a computer with Internet access is the easiest way to play CityVille, and practically any computer that can handle a graphical Web browser can handle the game. You might need to download a few extra programs and adjust some settings, though, and this chapter tells you how to do that.

After your computer is all set up for CityVille, you need to get connected to Facebook before you start working in your city. This chapter tells you how to set up a Facebook account or, if you already have one, how to install the CityVille application to make it playable from your existing Facebook account.

...equesting permission to do the fu...

Access my basic information

Includes name, profile picture, gender, n user ID, list of friends, and any other info I've shared with everyone.

 Send me email

CityVille may email me directly at simonsmom1979@hotmail.com · Change

 Post to my Wall

CityVille may post status messages, note photos, and videos to my Wall

...n, you agree to the CityVille **Terms of Service**

Getting Your Computer Set Up for CityVille

In contrast to most games on traditional gaming consoles, such as the Nintendo Wii or Sony PlayStation 3, CityVille is a Web-based game that you can play without inserting a disc or installing any programs to your hard drive. Your city and the game program required to maintain it exist as part of a series of online data centers maintained by CityVille's publisher, Zynga.

This means that you can employ practically any computer with an Internet connection and a graphical Web browser to play CityVille. We say "practically any computer" because the one you use needs to meet a few basic requirements for you to play CityVille on it.

You don't need the latest graphics card or expensive hardware to run CityVille, but the game may look smoother and run its animations more quickly on a more powerful machine.

Getting on the Internet

This book assumes that you're using a computer with Internet access. If you need help getting set up with an Internet connection and making your way around the Web, check out *The Internet For Dummies,* 12th Edition, by John R. Levine and Margaret Levine Young.

Although CityVille is playable on a dialup Internet connection, a broadband Internet connection greatly improves the speed and smoothness of your gaming experience.

Choosing a compatible Web browser

Because CityVille is a Web-based game, you need a Web browser to access it. Zynga suggests the following CityVille-compatible Internet browsers. All these browsers can be downloaded for free from their associated Web sites:

- ✔ **Google Chrome (Version 10):** www.google.com/chrome
- ✔ **Mozilla Firefox (Version 4):** www.mozilla.com/en-US/firefox
- ✔ **Apple Safari (Version 5):** www.apple.com/safari/download
- ✔ **Microsoft Internet Explorer (Version 9):** www.microsoft.com/
  windows/internet-explorer

Make sure that your browser has been updated to the latest version, which are in parentheses in the preceding list, before moving forward.

The Internet browser you're using may affect your CityVille game play! If you experience lags during game play, try switching browsers. If you're a regular Internet Explorer user, for example, try Google Chrome or another browser and see whether performance improves.

Getting the Adobe Flash Player

Your computer needs the Adobe Flash Player add-on for you to play CityVille. *Adobe Flash* is a multimedia platform that allows Web sites to include interactive and animated content, including games and videos.

You need the latest version of Adobe Flash Player, even if Flash Player is installed already. As of this writing, the latest version of Flash Player is 10. Follow the directions on the official Adobe Flash Player site at

```
http://get.adobe.com/flashplayer
```

Watch out for a couple of easy mistakes:

✔ Adobe offers a certified, virus-free version of its Flash Player for free at its Web site. Be wary of downloading the player from other sites that might request payment or include malicious software with your download.

✔ The free Flash Player is different from professional development tools, such as Adobe Flash Builder and Flash Professional. These tools cost money but aren't required to play CityVille.

✔ You must have administrator rights to be able to install Flash Player on a computer. In other words, you must be able to make changes to your computer, such as download software. If you will be playing on a borrowed computer, such as a work or school one, you can either request administrator rights to install it yourself or you will have to request that Flash Player be installed by your Information Technology (IT) department.

Enabling JavaScript

To play CityVille, you need to make sure that your browser has JavaScript enabled. *JavaScript* lets your browser talk to the CityVille servers and keep the city that you see on your screen synced with the version stored in the Internet "cloud" of online servers.

The following sections describe how to enable JavaScript on the various Web browsers that Zynga recommends for the game.

You need to follow the directions we provide here only if you've installed Abode Flash Player and the game doesn't load after you install it. In each case, the game should load properly after you complete the steps and reload the page.

Apple Safari

Enable JavaScript in Safari by following these steps:

1. **Click the Gears icon and on the drop-down list that appears, choose Preferences.**

   The Preference menu opens.

2. **Select the Security tab and then select the Enable JavaScript check box.**

3. **Click the red X in the upper-right corner of the menu.**

4. **Click the Refresh button in your browser window.**

Mozilla Firefox

Here's how to enable JavaScript in the Firefox browser:

1. **Choose Tools⇨Options.**

   The Options menu appears.

2. **Click the Content tab and on the menu that appears, select the Enable JavaScript check box.**

3. **Click OK and then click the Refresh button in your browser window.**

Internet Explorer

Enable JavaScript in Internet Explorer using these steps:

1. **Choose Tools⇨Internet Options.**

   The Tools menu is the one that looks like a gear on the top right of the window. The Internet Options menu appears.

2. **Select the Security tab and on the Security menu that appears, click the Internet icon (it looks like a globe) if it's not already selected.**

3. **Click the Custom Level button.**

   The Settings list appears.

4. **Scroll down to the Scripting section and click the Enable radio button under Active Scripting.**

5. **Click OK on the Settings list, click OK on the Security menu, and then click the Refresh button in your browser window.**

Chrome

Chrome automatically installs with JavaScript enabled, so you don't have to do anything.

Optimizing your performance

CityVille should run just fine after you install Flash Player and enable JavaScript. However, if you run into loading problems or other performance issues, such as lags in play or out-of-sync errors, here are a few things you can try to make your gaming experience run more smoothly:

- ✔ **Close other programs and browsers while playing CityVille.** Although having no other applications running isn't strictly necessary, it can definitely improve the stability of your computer and help prevent frequent crashing.

- ✔ **Select a lower graphics setting.** Clicking the Eye icon that appears in the Tools menu in the lower-right corner of the CityVille game area toggles the game's graphics between high and low quality. Low-quality graphics may look rougher, but should also make the game run faster.

   For more on using CityVille's Settings menu, see the section about navigating CityVille in Chapter 3.

- ✔ **Clear your cache.** The *cache* on your computer is a space in the hard drive where your computer saves Web sites you have visited. Clearing your cache improves game play by making your system run faster and more smoothly, as well as by making pages load faster.

How to clear your cache

The steps to clear your cache depend on your Web browser.

Apple Safari

Clear your cache in Safari by following these steps:

1. **Click the Gears icon on the top right of the page and on the drop-down list that appears, choose Reset Safari.**

   The Reset menu appears. All the items you can reset are checked by default. Deselect all except the Empty the Cache check box.

2. **Click the Reset button.**

   The message box disappears.

3. **Click the Refresh button in your browser window.**

Mozilla Firefox

Here's how to clear your cache in the Firefox browser:

1. **Choose Tools⇨Clear Recent History.**

   The Clear Recent History menu appears.

2. **Deselect all the boxes except the Cache check box.**

3. **Select the time range to clear from the drop-down menu.**

   Your options are Last Hour, Last 2 Hours, Last 4 Hours, Today, and Everything. We recommend selecting the Everything option.

4. **Click the Clear Now button.**

   The dialog box closes.

5. **Refresh your browser window.**

Internet Explorer

Clear your cache in Internet Explorer using these steps:

1. **Choose Tools⇨Internet Options.**

   The Tools menu is the one that looks like a gear on the top right of the window. The Internet Options menu appears.

2. **Click the General tab and on the menu that appears, click the Delete button under the Browsing History section in the middle of the box.**

   A new dialog box pops up showing you the different items you can delete.

3. **Deselect the Preserve Favorite Data check box and keep the other default boxes selected.**

   These default boxes are Temporary Internet Files, Cookies, and History.

4. **Click the Delete button, click the Apply button, and finally, click OK.**

   The dialog box closes.

5. **Click the Refresh button in your browser window.**

Chrome

You can clear your cache in Chrome using these steps:

1. **Click the Customize and Control Google Chrome button.**

   This menu is the one that looks like a wrench on the top right of the window. The Options menu appears in a new tab on your Web browser.

2. **Click the Under the Hood link on the right side of the page.**

   The Under the Hood options appear.

3. **Click the Clear Browsing Data button on the top.**

   The Clear Browsing Data dialog box appears.

4. **Deselect everything except the Empty the Cache check box.**

5. **Select the time range to clear from the Obliterate the following items from drop-down menu.**

   Your options are Last Hour, Last Day, Last 4 Weeks, and the Beginning of Time.

   Select the Beginning of Time option.

6. **Click the Clear Browsing Data button and then refresh your Web browser.**

   Click the gray X to the right of the tab's name at the top of your browser to close only this tab, or click the red X on the top right of your browser window to close your Internet window.

Creating a Facebook Account to Play the Game

If you're not already one of the 700 million (and growing) people with a Facebook account, you need to change that fact before jumping into CityVille. Luckily, signing up for Facebook is a free and easy process that shouldn't take long. Plus, signing up for Facebook can unlock a social journey. Just be careful of *oversharing*.

Although you may be tempted to post everything about you and your life on your new Facebook account, sharing too much personal information on the Internet, and especially on social networking sites like Facebook, can be dangerous. Don't include information like your physical address or home phone number in your profile unless you have a very compelling reason to do so, and strongly consider using Facebook's privacy controls to allow only your confirmed friends to view any updates you make to your profile.

To set up your Facebook account, follow these steps:

1. **In your preferred Web browser, go to www.facebook.com.**

   The Facebook sign-up/login page appears, as shown in Figure 2-1.

Facebook: A brief history

Social networking mega-site Facebook got its start at Harvard University in 2004. Facebook co-creator Mark Zuckerberg conceived of the site as a MySpace-style social network focused exclusively on letting college students connect and interact (although there's some controversy as to whether he devised the idea on his own). Although Harvard students were the first to have access to the site, the network quickly expanded to other colleges and then high schools and employers. Finally, in September 2006, anyone with a valid e-mail address could sign up for the site.

Although the functionality of the site was initially quite basic, features such as tagging, photo-sharing, and the now-ubiquitous Wall were introduced at a breakneck pace over the subsequent years. In May 2007, the introduction of the Facebook platform allowed third-party companies to build applications that integrated seamlessly with Facebook's social network, letting users connect with their friends in myriad new ways. This integration included games such as CityVille, which launched on the network in December 2010.

Although some users may feel that the current incarnation of Facebook has lost sight of the site's initial student-focused purpose, the majority of the 500 million current users would probably disagree. Now worth anywhere from $12 to $100 billion (depending on whose valuation of the private company you believe), the site continues to attract hundreds of thousands of new users daily and doesn't seem poised to stop growing any time soon.

Figure 2-1: The Facebook sign-up/login page.

2. **Sign up for your personal account by providing the following information:**

- *Your first and last names*

- *A valid e-mail address*

    Facebook doesn't share this address with the wider world if you don't want it to. You have to re-enter your e-mail address to confirm you typed it correctly.

- *A password*

    Choose something memorable but not obvious; *password,* for example, is *not* a good choice. Passwords that intersperse capital letters with lowercase ones, as well as with numbers or symbols, are much more secure than a simple series of letters or numbers.

- *Your sex:* Choose your sex from the I Am drop-down list.

- *Your birthday*

    Facebook doesn't allow users younger than 13 years of age. You can change your account settings to hide your birthday at any time by adjusting your privacy settings through the Account menu on the top right of your Facebook home page.

3. **Click the green Sign Up button.**

    A Security Check page appears, asking you to type a randomized set of words shown in a security image.

4. **Type the two security words shown in the text box and click the green Sign Up button.**

    The Find Friends page appears.

5. **(Optional) Enter the following requested information or click the Skip this Step link at the bottom of the page to continue without sharing this information with Facebook:**

    - *Find friends:* Enter your e-mail address and e-mail password; then click the Find Friends button to have Facebook automatically search for members who are already listed in your e-mail contacts. On the next screen, select the check boxes next to the contacts you want to add as Facebook friends. Then click the Add as Friends button.

    - *Profile information:* Enter the name of your high school, college or university, and employer. As you type, the Facebook network associated with each organization appears in a drop-down list. Select the appropriate network (and your class year, for the schools); then click the Save & Continue button to move on.

- *Profile picture:* Click the Upload a Photo link and then click the Choose File button to select a digital photo from your computer, or click the Take a Photo link and then the Save Picture button to capture your image via your webcam. Click Save & Continue when you're happy with your digital avatar.

6. **Check your e-mail for a confirmation message from Facebook and then click the link provided in the e-mail to confirm and validate your e-mail address.**

Congratulations! You're now among the newest members of Facebook. The very first thing you should do with your new account is edit your privacy settings. In the upper-right corner of the page, choose Account⇨Privacy Settings. From this page, you can control which of your personal details will be viewable by friends, friends of friends, or people on the Internet at large.

For more on protecting your Facebook privacy and getting the most from your new account, we recommend *Facebook For Dummies* by Carolyn Abram and Leah Pearlman.

After you have a Facebook account, you're ready to build your city!

Installing the CityVille App

If you've set up your Facebook account (see the preceding section for how to do that), you're almost ready to start enjoying life in your virtual city! Installing the CityVille app to your account is the only piece of business left to take care of before you can start the game, and it's an easy one.

Although you can also access the CityVille app through a Facebook search, an invitation from a Facebook friend, or the game's public-facing Facebook page, here's the most direct way to get the app installed to your Facebook account:

1. **Log in to your Facebook account by entering the e-mail address and password you used when signing up for your account; then click the Login button.**

If you're already logged in to Facebook, you can skip this step. See the "Creating a Facebook Account to Play the Game," section, earlier in this chapter, if you haven't yet obtained a Facebook account.

2. **Go to www.cityville.com.**

As of this writing CityVille doesn't have its own Web site, and the one provided here takes you directly to the CityVille Facebook Page.

3. **Click the blue Go to App button on the left side under the CityVille logo.**

The Request for Permission page appears, as shown in Figure 2-2.

Figure 2-2: The Request for Permission page.

4. **Click the blue Allow button so that CityVille can access the basic profile information on your Facebook account, send you e-mails, and post to your Wall.**

This information includes your name, profile picture, gender, networks, user ID, list of friends, and any other information you've shared with everyone via Facebook.

CityVille uses this information primarily to display your name and profile picture to your CityVille friends, and to tailor advertising opportunities to your expected interests.

By clicking the Allow button, you give CityVille permission to e-mail you directly with notifications about daily bonuses and neighbor requests pending.

After you complete the preceding steps, CityVille should load automatically; if it doesn't, make sure that you've installed the Adobe Flash Player and enabled JavaScript. (See the sections for performing each of these tasks earlier in this chapter.)

We cover details on how to start navigating your newly installed game in Chapter 3. The remainder of this chapter discusses how to best integrate CityVille into your normal Facebook activities and network of online friends.

Bookmarking CityVille on your Facebook account

Remembering to enter CityVille's URL into your browser's address box each time you want to play can quickly get annoying. Luckily, playing CityVille automatically adds the game to a Bookmarks sidebar on the left side of your Facebook home page, as shown in Figure 2-3. The exact position of CityVille on this list may change as you use other apps, but it jumps back to the top every time you play CityVille.

You can also bookmark CityVille using your Web browser.

Turning Facebook friends into CityVille neighbors

Starting a city can be lonely without anyone to be neighbors with, so the best way to jump-start your gaming experience is to add your existing Facebook friends to your CityVille game as neighbors. Neighbors are integral to the CityVille experience, as we discuss in more detail in Chapter 6. You can start with people who already play or invite those who don't to join. Asking friends who already play and sending invitations to those who don't is a great starting point for neighbor acquisition, and as a bonus, you're adding people you actually know!

CityVille neighbors make visiting and working in your city more fun and more productive by increasing your City Coins, Reputation Hearts, and Experience Points. Chapter 7 tells you more about earning City Coins and Experience Points, and Chapter 6 tells you more about the importance of Reputation Hearts.

Suggesting CityVille to friends

You can invite your Facebook friends to CityVille by accessing the Invite Friends or My Neighbors tabs found at the top of your CityVille home page. Your friends have to accept your invitation to play and must add you as a neighbor before they appear on your Neighbors list. The Invite tab triggers a list of all your Facebook friends. Scroll through the list and select the friends you want to invite. You can invite up to 40 friends at once.

Adding friends as neighbors

Maybe you already have some Facebook friends playing CityVille, but just don't know it. You can find out who plays and add them as neighbors by clicking the My Neighbors tab located at the top of your CityVille game's home page. All your Facebook friends who play CityVille automatically appear on the My Neighbors page. Now you can see who plays, but who isn't a neighbor yet. These friends are at the end of this list. Simply click the blue Add *[Friend Name]* as Neighbor button on the bottom right.

Figure 2-3: How the CityVille bookmark appears on the sidebar.

You can read all about the importance of neighbors and find out about additional ways to find neighbors in Chapter 6.

Staying Involved with CityVille Online

CityVille is everywhere! Well it's not *everywhere,* but you can easily interact with the people responsible for bringing you CityVille in many places online. These are great opportunities to chat with fellow players and to stay up to date on what's currently happening — and what's about to happen — in CityVille.

Twitter

Even if you're not active in the Twitterverse (catchy, isn't it?), it's hard to find a person these days who hasn't at least heard of the micro-blogging platform. C'mon, join in — everyone else is doing it! Give in to peer pressure! Forget what your parents used you tell you (at least in this instance!).

CityVille on Twitter

The Twitter username for CityVille is @zCityVille, which you can easily get to and start following by using this link:

```
http://twitter.com/zCityVille
```

The folks in charge of the account post frequent updates on what's happening in the world of virtual cities. In addition to following CityVille, you can find like-minded city slickers by searching for *CityVille* using the search bar at the top of your Twitter home page.

To help others find your CityVille-related tweets, make sure you note them with a *hashtag,* by typing the pound sign on your keyboard (#) before the word CityVille, such as #CityVille. Strike up conversations! Exchange tips and tricks! Interact with the people behind the @zCityVille account — they don't bite . . . that we know of.

Zynga on Twitter

In addition to following the CityVille account, you can also follow the Zynga Twitter account at @Zynga using this link:

```
http://twitter.com/#!/zynga
```

In addition to posts about your beloved CityVille, the account also tweets general Zynga news, which is especially helpful if you're active in other Zynga games, such as FarmVille. It's the same as with the CityVille account: Search for *Zynga* using the search bar at the top of your Twitter home page to pull up tweets that mention the word *Zynga*. When you send an update — whether it's about Zynga, CityVille, or both — be sure to include hashtags (#) so others can find you.

Zynga: A brief history

In June of 2007, Mark Pincus started *Zynga,* the online gaming company responsible for not only CityVille, but also FarmVille, Mafia Wars, and Zynga Poker. In all, Zynga has 19 games for Facebook, 7 for MySpace, 5 for the iPhone, and 3 for Yahoo!.

Pincus named the company after his late American Bulldog, Zinga, and the company chose a bulldog as its logo. The name represents a "loyal and spirited" character and is modeled after a late African Warrior queen. The company is headquartered in San Francisco, CA, and has offices all over the world including India, Beijing, Toyko, and Frankfurt in addition to their U.S.-based offices.

Over the last three years, Zynga has grown by leaps and bounds. In 2010 alone, Zynga acquired at least four other gaming companies and boasted more than 1,300 employees in all the locations. CityVille is its strongest game yet. When CityVille debuted in December 2010, it overtook FarmVille as Zynga's most popular game with more than 5 million daily users within its first month. As of this writing, more than 20 million people check in on their cities daily, and nearly 100 million check in at least once a month.

Facebook

CityVille has its own Facebook Page! Yes, we're pretty darn excited about that, too. What better place to discuss a Facebook-based game than on Facebook? As we mention earlier, as of this writing CityVille does not have its own Web site outside of Facebook, but that may change in the future. The Page can be found at www.cityville.com and is updated more frequently than its Twitter account at the moment. When new features, such as buildings and decorations, are added, this is the place to find out about them right away. What's even better is that updates include helpful links to take you directly to the game so you don't even have to lift a finger, besides the one you use to click your mouse, that is.

While you're on the CityVille Facebook Page, click the Like button at the top of the Page.

Be sure to check out all the tabs at the top of the Page (see Figure 2-4):

- ✔ The **Wall tab** is where game updates, such as new items in the Build menu, are found.
- ✔ The **Info tab** is where you can find background information on Zynga and CityVille including links to their Twitter account and forums.

✔ The **Reviews tab** shows you the many people that love CityVille, and believe us, there's a whole lot of love for CityVille!

While you're there, why don't you write a review of your own to add to the list?

✔ The **Play Now! tab** provides a big (and we mean *big*) button that takes you to the game.

✔ The **Zynga Games tab** contains pictures and links to Zynga's other games — the better to get you addicted to even more Zynga titles, of course!

If you ever get lost and need to find your way back to CityVille, all the important links are listed on the left side of the Page. This includes links to the game, to the official forums (discussed in the next section), and to the CityVille Twitter account.

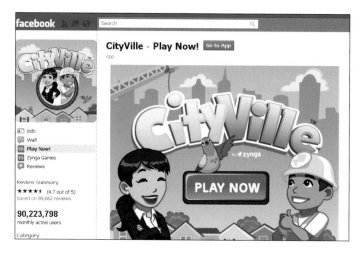

Figure 2-4: The CityVille Facebook Page.

Official CityVille forums

We talk about forums more in Chapter 6, but we thought you might want to dive in as soon as you get started with the game. The official forums are run and managed by the folks behind CityVille and are found at `http://zyn.ga/1nV`.

For the rest of this chapter, we point out a few of the important forums that are worth taking a look at now and again.

The CityVille Forum Guide forum near the bottom with a megaphone icon to the left of it gives the lay of the land as far as the CityVille forums are concerned.

You *know* it's important if a megaphone's involved!

This forum goes into detail about what each forum *thread,* or topic, is for. For example, this section explains that the Hear Ye! Hear Ye! forum is the place to visit for all the latest CityVille news.

Here are the available forums:

City Regulations

The City Regulations forum is where all of the official Zynga "housekeeping" is covered, such as rules regarding creating a signature under your forum name and that you can't have multiple accounts as per Zynga's Terms of Service agreement.

Hear Ye! Hear Ye!

Hear Ye! Hear Ye! is where you find out about the latest happenings in the world of virtual cities, such as new quests being added and new Build Menu items to watch out for. Be sure to check back often because Zynga is always making improvements to the game. See Figure 2-5 for a look at some typical posts in the Heat Ye! Hear Ye! forum.

Figure 2-5: The variety of posts in the Hear Ye! Hear Ye! forum

City Map

The City Map forum is divided into two sub-forums:

- ✔ **City Council Guides** includes helpful posts by the forum leaders. These include topics, such as the Guide to Neighbor Visitation Bonuses and the Guide to Trains. Figure 2-6 shows some guides explaining new features of CityVille. If you ever find yourself confused about a new item or feature of the game, head on over to this sub-forum to get more information.

- ✔ **City Builder Guides** are posted by forum members like you. These include topics, such as a Quest List and a Master Collections List.

City Builder Guides are likely to change, and some of the information included may not be up to date.

Figure 2-6: The official City Council Guides from Zynga under the City Map forum.

The Help Desk

The Help Desk forum includes two sub-forums run by fellow CityVille players. Because these are sub-forums where fellow users publish answers, you're more likely to find differing opinions on answers, so you have to pick and choose what advice to follow:

- ✔ The **Frequently Asked Questions sub-forum** is exactly what it sounds like — a list of answers to questions that get asked frequently. You're encouraged to check this sub-forum before submitting a question to the Ask a New Question sub-forum.

- ✔ The **Ask a New Question sub-forum** is also pretty self-explanatory.

These players can be very helpful because they're on the front lines, so to speak. You're also likely to get a quick answer to your question.

Town Square

The Town Square forum is where Zynga gives the power to the people — as long as it's within forum regulations, of course! Town Square is divided into two sub-forums:

- **City Hall** where you can chat about everything CityVille with your fellow players. In February 2011, a moderator created a thread in City Hall asking how CityVille has made it easier to connect with friends from around the world. Many users responded — maybe you should head on over and post your own story!

- **Playground** where you can connect with other players. The topics here don't have to be centered on CityVille. Just remember to follow the rules!

Bug Reporting and Known Issues

Sometimes, software doesn't work the way it's supposed to. These forums give you a voice for speaking and an ear for listening:

- The **Known Issues sub-forum** is a great place to ease your mind and assure yourself that you're not going crazy, and that there really *is* something screwy going on with your game. The folks behind the scenes in this forum stay on top of any technical issues players may be having and, if necessary, refer them to a different forum and thread for the answer.

- If for some reason you experience a completely unique issue that isn't addressed anywhere in the forums, head on over to the **Bug Reporting sub-forum** where you can add your suspected bug to an existing thread.

Proposals and Feedback

Do you have the perfect idea for a CityVille addition? We mean the *perfect* idea? By all means, let Zynga know! Zynga welcomes your ideas for changes and additions to CityVille. After all, everyone wants the game to be the best it can be, right? If you have an opinion on an existing feature, the Feedback sub-forum is for you.

Play nice! Rude, obscene, or off-color comments will be removed.

Cityscaping

Not everyone can be a professional landscaper or city planner in real life. But there sure are some good ones hanging around CityVille! The Cityscaping forum is the place to go to see screenshots of other players' cities. Cityscaping is a great place to not only gather ideas for how to lay out your city, but who knows, maybe you'll also get a sneak peek of some items from the Build menu that aren't available yet.

Add New Neighbors

This forum is for exactly what the name implies — adding new neighbors. You may not realize this quite yet, but neighbors are a must-have addition in CityVille! Head on over to this forum if you're looking to give a boost to your neighbor bar. People from all over the world post messages if they're looking to add new neighbors and meet new people in the process! You can post one "add me" request per day. For more information on adding neighbors, see Chapter 6.

3

Navigating CityVille

In This Chapter

▶ Navigating the CityVille menus

▶ Keeping track of your city's statistics

▶ Visiting the neighbor bar

*E*veryone's gotten lost while driving through an unfamiliar city at some point, right? How frustrating that is! It seems that all you have to do is make one incorrect move, and you're completely thrown off course and it takes forever to find your way back. Although no one has ever ventured into CityVille and never been heard from again, there are a few tools and menus you need to know to build your thriving metropolis.

In this chapter, we introduce you to the handy options available, such as CityVille menus, as well as the tools of the trade you need to build your city. Let this chapter be your GPS system to the virtual neighborhoods of CityVille!

Navigating CityVille

Before you place buildings and beautify your city, you have to figure out how to use the buttons and tools that let you control your space. The CityVille user interface (UI) may look complicated, but after you know what everything does, it won't seem so bad, we promise. The major portions of the UI, and the names used to refer to them, are shown in Figure 3-1 and detailed in the next section.

Figure 3-1: The major parts of the CityVille user interface.

Using the Top menu

The Top menu consists of eight gold tabs and the CityVille Messages tab located above the CityVille play area. The following sections explain the items on the Top menu and what you can access by clicking them.

The Free Gifts tab

Clicking the Free Gifts tab redirects you to the CityVille gifting page, as shown in Figure 3-2, where you can select free gifts to send to your neighbors (for more on meeting and interacting with CityVille neighbors, see Chapter 6).

Though the specific items on the gifting page differ for each city dweller and occasionally change throughout the year, the page always includes a variety of decorations, as well as batteries for Energy, zoning permits, and supplies to help your friends complete seasonal goals. We get into more detail about the uses for each of these gifts in later chapters.

To send a gift, follow these steps:

1. **Select the radio button under the gift you want to give.**

2. **Click the Proceed to Send button to bring up the recipient selection screen.**

Figure 3-2: The CityVille gifting page.

3. **Select the check boxes for any number of friends to whom you want to send the gift.**

4. **Click the Send Gift Request button to send.**

 On the recipient selection screen, you can type a name in the Start Typing a Name box to jump straight to a specific Facebook friend. In addition, you can limit the list to fellow CityVille players among your Facebook friends by clicking the CityVille Friends tab at the top of the list.

 Some free gifts may have a Padlock icon next to their pictures. This means that you haven't reached a high enough level or you do not have enough neighbors to be able to send that gift yet. (For more on attaining higher levels, see Chapter 7.)

Although sending gifts featured on the gifting page is free, you can send only one gift every four hours per Facebook friend. If you find that a neighbor's name is missing from the list, you've recently sent them a gift and have to wait to send them another one.

The Play tab

The Play tab is the most important tab on the Top menu. Clicking the Play tab always redirects you to the play area for your city, where you can do everything from setting up buildings to harvesting crops. For more about interacting with your city using the Play tab, see the rest of the book.

The My Neighbors tab

Clicking the My Neighbors tab brings up the My Neighbors page, as shown in Figure 3-3. This page shows you everything you need to know about your current Facebook friends who play CityVille.

> ✔ Each CityVille-playing friend is grouped into one of three categories:
>
> • Neighbors
>
> • Pending neighbor requests
>
> • Non-neighbors
>
> ✔ You can also see each friend's current CityVille status for
>
> • Level
>
> • Experience Points (XP)
>
> • Coins

Figure 3-3: The My Neighbors page.

You can use the buttons on this page to

> ✔ Invite your other Facebook friends to CityVille.
>
> ✔ Send a neighbor request to friends who play CityVille but aren't neighbors yet.

✔ Remove inactive neighbors from your Neighbors list.

✔ Send gifts to both neighbors and non-neighbors, as we detail in the "The Free Gifts tab" section earlier in this chapter.

To invite your other Facebook friends to CityVille using the My Neighbors tab, follow these steps:

1. **In the Start Typing a Name box, type the name, or the first few letters of the name, of the friend you want to invite.**

   Facebook immediately shows you names that match your search inquiry.

   You can also click the gray arrows on the right side of the page to scroll through the list of friends to find those you want to invite.

2. **Select the check box next to the name of the person you want to invite.**

   This adds them to your invitation list located right above the blue Send CityVille Invitation button.

3. **Click the Send CityVille Invitation button**.

   A preview of the message that's sent to your friend appears. You can add a personal message to it by clicking the Add Personal Message link on the top left, underneath the recipient's names.

4. **After you have the message the way you want, click Send; or if you decide against inviting this person, click Cancel.**

If your neighbors have added items to their inventory's wish list, those items display next to their photos on this tab as well. (For more on the wish list, see the "Looking at your stuff with the My Stuff menu" section later in this chapter.) Be careful about gifting items in this manner, though. The item that you send will be removed from your inventory! If you don't have any of the items on their list, that item's Gift button is grayed out.

You can't cancel pending neighbor requests at this time. For more on interacting with neighbors, see Chapter 6. See Chapter 7 for more information on inventories.

The My Neighbors page is the only place to remove deadbeat neighbors that have become inactive city dwellers, so remember to use it to keep your Neighbors list lean and pruned. Doing so will only help you in the long run! To remove a neighbor from your list, click the red Delete button on the right of the page.

You aren't shown a separate deletion confirmation button, so make sure you really want to delete this neighbor! If you accidentally delete a neighbor or decide you want one back, you have to resend a neighbor invitation — which he may choose not to accept!

The Invite Friends tab

Inviting your Facebook friends who don't play CityVille to join in the fun using the Invite Friends tab is the same as using the My Neighbors tab:

1. **In the Start Typing a Name box, type the name, or the first few letters of the name, of the friend you want to invite.**

   Facebook immediately shows you names that match your search inquiry.

   You can also click the gray arrows on the right side of the page to scroll through the list of friends to find those you want to invite.

2. **Select the check box next to the name of the person you want to invite.**

   This adds them to your invitation list located right above the blue Send CityVille Invitation button.

3. **Click the Send CityVille Invitation button.**

   A preview of the message that's sent to your friend appears. You can add a personal message to it by clicking the Add Personal Message link underneath the recipient's names.

4. **After you have the message the way you want, click Send; or if you decide against inviting this person, click Cancel.**

Zynga makes it easy for you to find the perfect neighbors by giving you tabs to help you sort your options into the categories My Active Zynga Friends (friends who play other Zynga games), All Friends, CityVille Friends (those who play but who aren't your neighbor yet), and an optional tab that appears only if you currently play another Zynga game. For example, if you're a FarmVille player, a FarmVille Friends tab appears.

Even if a Facebook friend accepts your invitation to play CityVille here, she doesn't appear as one of your CityVille neighbors until she accepts your neighbor request. See Chapter 6 for more on sending and accepting neighbor requests.

The Add Coins & Cash tab

Clicking the Add Coins & Cash tab on the Top menu brings up a page where you can purchase in-game currency — City Cash and City Coins — using real world currency. You use in-game currency to buy

✔ Items like buildings, decorations, and Energy Batteries

✔ Land expansion permits that allow you to expand your city far and wide

To purchase City Cash and City Coins, follow these steps:

1. **While on the Add Coins and Cash tab, click the radio button next to the amount of City Cash or City Coins you want to purchase.**

2. **Click the green Continue button.**

3. **Select how you want to pay and then fill in the appropriate information.**

   The payment options are through PayPal or credit cards (such as MasterCard and Visa), or you can charge the amount to your cellphone or home phone bill using one of the outside vendors featured underneath the blue CityVille box on this page. If you chose to add the charges to your phone bill, you're taken away from the Zynga Web site to complete your transaction.

   Cellphone service providers support different purchase options, so you may have to spend more than you originally intended. Be sure to thoroughly check out this option before selecting it.

4. **Click the blue Buy City Cash! button if paying by PayPal or credit cards.**

   Your CityVille account is automatically credited the amount of currency you purchased. If you have problems or questions, contact Zynga directly using the information in Chapter 10.

The Earn City Cash tab

Clicking the Earn City Cash tab brings you to a menu with a number of third-party offers you can sign up for to earn some City Cash. These options can be anything from purchasing magazine subscriptions to signing up for DVD rental services. The company offering the deal decides on the amount of City Cash you receive when you complete the offer, and that number is clearly printed on the big gold Sign Up button to the right of the offer. Click this button to go to the Web site of the company making the offer to complete the transaction. After you complete the offer, City Cash appears in your CityVille account.

Zynga and Facebook don't operate these offers, so if you run into any issues, you must contact the company directly.

Use your best judgment when completing these offers. If you have never heard of a company and the offer seems too good to be true — do more research into the company before spending your hard-earned "real world" money.

The GameCards tab

The GameCards tab is for those lucky people who have a Zynga *Game Card,* which is a prepaid gift card purchased from retailers like Walmart, Best Buy, Walgreens, or Rite Aid.

To find a retailer near you, click the pull-down menu in the gray bar in the center of the GameCards screen directly above the retailer's logos. Currently, Game Cards are sold only in the United States, Canada, and the United Kingdom. The cards have no value until they're activated at the cash register.

On this tab, you can cash in your Game Card by entering the pin code found on the back of the Game Gard's packaging. After the card validation process is complete, your Zynga player account is credited the amount of the card and you can use that money to purchase City Cash or Coins.

The Help tab

Need help with CityVille? Check out the Help tab. This page has a helpful rundown of the game's main components as well as a Frequently Asked Questions (FAQ) section. If your question isn't answered with the information presented, you can click the CityVille Forums link at the top of the page or the Customer Support link at the bottom of the page.

Of course, you could just look in the book you're currently holding. See Chapter 10 for more information on other Web resources that can provide you the CityVille help you need.

The CityVille Messages tab

The rightmost tab at the top of the CityVille play area is the CityVille Messages tab, represented by a white tab with a red Z on it. The white number at the top-right corner of the tab represents the number of unread messages that you have. If you don't have any messages, 0 displays.

Click the tab to bring up the CityVille messages page, which lists an assortment of in-game events that require action on your part. These include CityVille gifts sent to you by other players, neighbor invitations, and requests for help in neighboring cities (see Figure 3-4). Accepting each request is as simple as clicking the button next to its description. You can also sort your requests and gifts by clicking the applicable headings on the top left, directly above the messages.

Figure 3-4: The CityVille messages page.

If you have messages, the content of this tab appears automatically when you get to your game screen. Even if you have no messages, you can still click the tab to send free gifts to your neighbors or to head directly to your city to play.

 You can also view your CityVille messages by clicking the Game Requests link or the CityVille link on the left side of your Facebook home page. Note that the Game Requests link appears only if you have messages waiting for you; however, the CityVille link is always available for you to click to get back to your city.

 CityVille requests don't last forever — in fact, they expire if you don't answer them within a month. Neighbor help requests last only as long as it takes for that neighbor to get the help he needs, whether from you or another neighbors. If the request has already been satisfied, a message says as much when you click the button.

After a gift request has been accepted, however, the item remains in your in-game's inventory indefinitely, so be sure to click the Accept and Play button as soon as possible, even if you don't plan on using the gift just yet. Once you have accepted each request, click the white box with the blue X on the top right of this dialog box to close it.

Setting graphics and sound options with the Settings menu

 The Settings menu is the little gear icon located in the bottom right of the CityVille playing area, right above your neighbor bar.

✔ Click the gear icon to bring up the following Settings menu.

✔ Click the gear icon again to collapse the menu.

The Settings menu features the following six options:

- ✔ **Zoom Out:** Clicking the Magnifying Glass icon with the minus sign zooms out your view, so you see the city from higher in the air.

  Use this view to see the unclaimed land available for future expansions or to decrease the amount of moving around the screen you have to do.

- ✔ **Zoom In:** Clicking the Magnifying Glass icon with the plus sign takes you out of the zoomed-out view and back to the default view.

- ✔ **Toggle Graphics Quality:** Clicking the Eye icon lets you choose between high- and low-resolution graphics.

  Although running with lower-quality graphics means in-game items have a rougher appearance and more jagged edges, it also may help CityVille run more smoothly.

  Try turning down the quality to see whether it helps your playing experience. When the button is a darker blue, the lower-resolution graphics are shown.

- ✔ **Toggle Full Screen:** Clicking the icon with the two rectangles lets you expand your view so your CityVille play area takes up your entire computer screen.

  Use this view to get the overall picture of your city.

  To go back to the normal view, click the Toggle Full Screen button again or press the Esc key on your keyboard.

- ✔ **Sound On/Off:** Clicking the Speaker icon toggles the sound effects in your city — including the clinking sounds when you collect from your stores and the sound of Experience Points being added to your XP meter.

- ✔ **Music On/Off:** Clicking the Music Note icon toggles the cheerful CityVille music.

Keeping track of your city's stats

There are two other displays that you need to be familiar with to build and maintain a successful city. These areas are the meat and potatoes of your progress in the game, if you will.

The five stat counters, as shown in Figure 3-5, can make or break your ability to grow your mega-metropolis to earth-shattering dimensions. If you don't keep an eye on these meters, you run the risk of running out of money and Energy to perform important tasks like harvesting crops, collecting from businesses, or running out of Goods to supply your businesses. Consider it the control center for the status of your city.

Figure 3-5: The stats bar.

Here is what the items on the stats bar are all about:

- **Coin display:** Displays your current amount of City Coins. Note that this number updates in real time as you buy items, collect from your buildings, harvest crops, and receive bonuses. Every city runner starts the game with 7,000 Coins. For more on obtaining and spending City Coins, see Chapter 7.

- **City Cash display:** Displays your current amount of City Cash. This number updates in real time as well, and each city starts with 5 Cash. For more on obtaining and spending City Cash, see Chapter 7.

- **Energy meter and counter:** This meter next to the lightning bolt shows you how much Energy you have to perform many common city tasks. These tasks include collecting from buildings, harvesting crops, and building homes and businesses.

   The easiest way to get more Energy is to simply wait — every five minutes you earn one more Energy in your meter, even if you aren't actively playing the game at the time. The countdown clock above the meter shows how long until you earn one more Energy.

   You can store only a certain maximum amount of Energy at any time. Every city slicker starts with a meter that holds a maximum of 12 Energy. This number increases by 1 every time you earn a new level by collecting Experience Points. If your Energy meter is full, you can't gain more Energy by waiting for the countdown clock, using items, or helping neighbors. See Chapter 7 for more information on managing your Energy levels and Chapter 6 for more information about increasing your reputation count.

- **Goods meter:** The purple meter next to the Box icon tells you how many Goods you have to supply your businesses with. These Goods are used to replenish businesses and get them serving customers again.

   Every city starts with 100 Goods and has a maximum storage capacity of 715 Goods. Storage buildings, such as Barns and Silos, are available for purchase and increase the amount of Goods that can be stored. For more information on Goods and storage, see Chapter 7.

   Hover your mouse pointer over the Goods meter to show the current maximum Goods storage capacity for your city.

✔ **Experience Points meter:** The rightmost area on the stats bar is your Experience Points (XP) and level counter. Every city starts at Level 1 with 0 XP. You can earn XP by clicking the Star icons that appear when you perform certain city tasks, as discussed in detail in Chapter 7. When you've collected enough XP, you earn a new level, which can unlock certain items.

If you hover your mouse over this counter, you can see the number of XP needed to reach the next level.

Visiting your neighbor bar

The bar of neighbors' faces lining the bottom of the CityVille play area isn't just there to make you feel less lonely. This bar lists all your CityVille neighbors, organized from left to right according to their level in the game.

Click the arrows on either side of the bar to scroll the list in that direction:

✔ The single arrow moves the list one neighbor at a time.

✔ The double arrows move the list four neighbors at a time.

✔ The arrow with a vertical line moves the list ten neighbors at a time.

Clicking a neighbor's name or picture on this bar brings up a menu letting you send gifts or visit and help your neighbor's city. For more on interacting with neighbors using these options, see Chapter 6.

Getting to Know the Menus

Now's the time to introduce you to the different menus you use throughout your time in CityVille. These are more than just neat-looking pictures at the bottom of your play screen! We get into details about when and where you should use a specific tool and what to expect when you click a particular icon.

Once you're finished reading this section, you'll be perusing your inventory and moving objects with the best of them!

Using the Tools menu

The Tools menu is located in the bottom-right corner of the CityVille play area, next to your neighbor bar, as shown in Figure 3-6. You use these tools to move existing objects and buildings around your city, rotate buildings to fit your needs, remove objects — basically, just about everything! Knowing how to use each of these tools is crucial to creating and maintaining your virtual city, so we dive right in:

- ✔ **Pointer tool:** Click the black arrow in the upper-left corner of the menu area to select the Pointer tool. This is the default cursor you use for the most basic actions in CityVille — collecting profits from businesses, collecting rent from houses, planting crops, and moving the viewpoint around so you can see different areas of your city. Unless otherwise noted, when we tell you to click something in this book, we mean to click it with the Pointer tool selected.

  To view different sections of your city that may not be visible in your game play area, simply click and drag the pointer with your mouse.

  If you're using any of the other tools and want to return to the Pointer tool, simply click the red circle with the slash through it that replaced the black arrow on the menu.

  Clicking the Pointer Tool icon expands the Tools menu and gives access to three more options:

- ✔ **Remove tool:** Click the Backhoe icon to choose the Remove tool, which can be used to quickly sell any item in your city for City Coins. Simply click to choose the tool, click the item you want to sell, and then click Yes to confirm the sale.

  Don't automatically click Yes to confirm your sale, or else you may permanently lose an exclusive item that can be hard or impossible to reacquire. Make sure you're deleting the item you think you're deleting before moving on.

  Selling items using the Remove tool gets you considerably less than what you paid for them. For example, purchasing the Apartment Building from the Build menu costs you 4,500 City Coins, yet selling it brings in only about 225 Coins.

- ✔ **Rotate tool:** Click the Gold icon that looks like two arrows going in a circle and then click any building to rotate it:

  - • Dwellings, such as houses and apartment buildings, can be rotated 360 degrees.

  - • Businesses can be rotated only 180 degrees.

  You can rotate some decorations, but many decorations look the same from every angle.

Figure 3-6: The Tools menu.

✔ **Move tool:** Click the gray multi-arrow icon at the top of the Tools menu to choose the Move tool. With the Move tool selected, click any building or decoration in your city to pick it up, and then move the mouse and click again to place it in a new location.

Two objects can't share the exact same location. If the object you're holding appears slightly translucent and has a red box showing underneath it, at least part of it overlaps with another object. Try dropping the object back in its original location and then clearing some space in your planned location before trying to move the item again. You can also click the red circle with a slash through it in the menu area to drop the object back in its original location. When a location is free and clear for you to place a held object, a green square appears underneath the object, as shown in Figure 3-7.

Figure 3-7: A correct object placement.

Dwellings and stores need to be adjacent to the street or a sidewalk to be effective. Although you can place these buildings in other locations, a red circle with a slash appears through the building to indicate that it isn't connected. See Chapter 5 for more information on placing buildings effectively, and Chapters 4 and 9 for more information on placing decorations.

Looking at your stuff with the My Stuff menu

The My Stuff menu is located on the bottom right of the play area, to the right of the Tools menu. This menu is symbolized by the image of a green present and a brown cardboard box. Clicking this button brings up access to menus, as shown in Figure 3-8, that keep track of your franchises, inventory, and collections:

- ✔ **The Franchise menu:** This menu is your dashboard for running your franchise stores in your neighbor's cities, which we discuss in more detail in Chapter 6. This dialog box is where you collect your store's daily proceeds and supply your franchise stores with Goods. If your neighbor hasn't accepted your latest franchise Goods delivery, you can also click the orange Remind button to post a reminder message to your neighbors' Wall, asking them to open their stores.

- ✔ **The Inventory menu:** The Inventory dialog box, as shown in Figure 3-9, is found by clicking the brown cardboard Inventory box in the center of the My Stuff menu. Whenever you receive a gift from a friend or earn an item by trading in a collection, that item is stored in your inventory. Items that you purchase, such as decorations and buildings, must be placed in your city right away and can't be collected in your inventory.

The tiny white number on the bottom right of each item in your inventory shows how many of that item you currently have. You can have a maximum of 2,000 total items in your inventory. After you reach the limit, you can't collect any other items until you use up existing ones.

Figure 3-8: Check out your stuff in the My Stuff menu.

Figure: 3-9: Keep track of the items in your inventory.

Inventory items received as rewards for trading in a collection can be used at any time — just click the item's image in your inventory to use it (in the case of Energy Batteries) or to place it in your city (in the case of decorations). If you have more than one of a certain type of item, you can use them each separately.

Not all inventory items are usable in this manner, though. Certain items like zoning permits, city seals, and gold plating stay in your inventory until you need them to complete a task, such as finishing a Community Building. These items are used automatically when they're needed, but you can still keep track of your current storage in the Inventory dialog box.

Your *wish list* displays at the top of the Inventory dialog box. If you need a certain item to complete a collection, finish building a Community Building, or help you play the game, you can add that item to your wish list by clicking the paper with the green + icon on the bottom right of that item's image. You can have a maximum of five distinct items in your wish list at one time.

After you set up your wish list, you can share it with your neighbors by clicking the green Share button at the top of the page. This posts a message on your Facebook Wall saying that you need help completing a collection.

✏ **Collections:** Click the trophy Collections button at the top of the My Stuff menu to bring up the Collections dialog box, as shown in Figure 3-10. Here, you can see the collectible items you've collected by performing tasks, such as harvesting crops and collecting from your businesses:

- *If you have not collected a particular collectible,* that image appears faded out.

- *If you have collected at least one of a collectible,* the image is in full color and has a small white number on the bottom right, displaying how many of that item that you have.

- *If you don't have enough collectibles for the reward,* the Trade In button is gray.

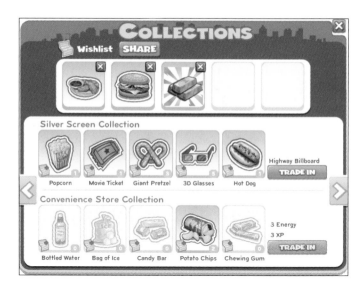

Figure 3-10: Viewing all your collections.

- *After you find all the collectibles from a certain collection,* the Trade In button on the right side of the page turns green and becomes clickable.

Click the Trade In button to exchange one set of that collection for the displayed reward, which can be anything from Energy points to Experience Points to decorations to place around your city. Chapter 7 gives you more information on how to utilize collections.

If you complete a collection that gives you extra Energy points or Goods, don't necessarily trade it in right away. Save it for a time when you're running too low on Energy or Goods to complete an important task.

4

Using the Build Menu

In This Chapter

▶ Getting a grip on the Build menu

▶ Increasing population, earning money, and collecting Goods

▶ Raising your population cap

▶ Getting more with Energy and expansions

▶ Improving your city

At its core, CityVille is primarily a game about making and spending money to continually expand the size of your city and increase its assets. Chapter 7 explains the types of currency used in CityVille and how to gain more by purchasing it with real money or by other means, such as increasing your level. In this chapter, you find out to how to go about spending your CityVille currency on necessary purchases: the houses, stores, decorations, and other essential items for running and expanding your city. You buy all these essentials through the Build menu, which we thoroughly describe in this chapter. Also in this chapter are a few basic tips for keeping to a set play schedule and managing your money and Energy wisely.

The Build Menu: Where It All Begins

The Build menu, as shown in Figure 4-1, is the hub for all your purchases in CityVille. You can access this menu by clicking the Build icon in the Tools menu, which you find in the lower-right corner of the play area.

To view the various product sections of the CityVille Build menu, do one of the following:

✔ Click the tabs at the top of the Build menu.

✔ Click the right and left arrows on either side of the menu to scroll through the pages of the current product section.

Figure 4-1: The Housing tab of the Build menu.

Each item listing on the Build menu contains the item's name and cost, which displays in either City Coins or City Cash, depending on the item. There is additional information available when you hover your mouse over the item listing; however, the specific information depends on what tab of the Build menu you're in. For example, if you're in the Housing tab, you see how much your population will increase when you build the home, the amount of rent you will collect, and the minimum amount of time between rent collections.

Not all items in the Build menu are available at all times; many are locked until you achieve a certain level, attract a certain number of neighbors, or complete a certain goal. If these requirements are unmet, they're clearly marked on the item's button, as shown in Figure 4-2. Hover your mouse over the item to get more information about it, such as which goal you have to complete to unlock it. When indicated, you can also unlock some items ahead of schedule by spending City Cash.

Figure 4-2: Examples of locked items in the Build menu.

Items in the CityVille Build menu fall into two general categories:

- ✓ **Tangible:** Items that can be physically placed on your city.
- ✓ **Consumable:** Items that you purchase, such as Energy, which are added to your Energy supply right away.

When you click the picture of a tangible Build item, the Build menu disappears and you return to your city, where you can place that item (or plant the seed) with a click of the mouse. Note that the purchase price for these tangible items isn't deducted from your account until you actively place that item on your city. Don't worry too much about placement — you can always move these items later with the Move tool.

If you change your mind about a tangible purchase after clicking the Buy button or simply can't find an open place to put your item, don't panic — just click the red circle with the slash through it in the Tools menu to cancel your pending purchase without spending any in-game currency.

Although you can purchase most decorations from the Build menu, CityVille has some items that you can earn only as free gifts.

Increasing Population with Housing

People make the world go 'round, right? At least they do in CityVille! Without a healthily growing population, your stores won't provide some much-needed currency and you can't advance in the game because many items are unlocked only after you have a certain number of people in your city. Besides, isn't it fun watching all your residents scurry around your city like little ants?

You increase your population by building homes for them to live in. Simple, huh? It's one of those "if you build it, they will come" situations. The larger the home, the more people it will add to your overall population — there's no such thing as abandoned buildings in CityVille.

There's a catch, though. You will notice two numbers underneath your city's name on the upper left of your neighbor bar. The first number is the total number of people you currently have living in your city. The second number is the maximum number of people you can have based on how many community buildings you have in your city. This is referred to as your *population cap.* The more community buildings you have, the higher your population cap is. To progress through the game, you have to keep adding community buildings to your city. We talk more about this later in this chapter in the section "Raising Your Population Cap with Community Buildings."

Now that that's out of the way, you can get started on building houses to increase your population. When you begin the game and complete the short tutorial, you have three houses available for purchase using City Coins — the Cozy Cottage, the Family Townhouse, and the Skyscraper Condos — whereas the Lake House can be purchased with City Cash. As you move through the game and complete goals, increase your population, gain Experience Points, and get more neighbors, more homes become available to you. Chapter 9 discusses how to choose the right housing to make it the city of your dreams.

First, you have to build these homes! Click the Housing tab in the Build menu to display a listing of all the available homes you can build in your city, as shown in Figure 4-1. Each listing shows a picture of the home and how much it costs. If you hover your mouse over the image, you see the following information:

- The population increase you get by placing the home
- The amount of rent you collect from the home
- The amount of time until you can collect rent

You can click the right and left arrows on the sides of the menu to see more homes for sale. We discuss building and placing homes in Chapter 5.

Zynga adds new homes frequently as it continues to develop the game, but Table 4-1 shows the homes available for purchase as of this writing.

Table 4-1		Housing Options on the Build Menu				
Name	**Cost**	**Population**	**Rent**	**Collection Time**	**Requirements**	**Size**
Cozy Cottage	200 Coins	10	50	1 hour	None	3 x 3
Family Townhouse	400 Coins	20	100	4 hours	None	4 x 4
Country Home	600 Coins	30	10	5 minutes	None	4 x 4
Suburban House	800 Coins	40	180	18 hours	Level 4 or 4 City Cash	4 x 4
Loft Apartments	1,000 Coins	50	220	2.1 days	Level 5 or 5 City Cash	4 x 4
Spring Bungalow	9,000 Coins	72	130	2 hours	Level 9 or 9 City Cash	3 x 3

Name	Cost	Population	Rent	Collection Time	Requirements	Size
Modern Chateau	1,500 Coins	60	200	1 day	Goal: Build a Burger Joint	4 x 4
Lake House	10 City Cash	90	180	2 hours	None	3 x 3
Terraced Brownstone	2,500 Coins	70	150	8 hours	Level 10 or 10 City Cash	3 x 3
Stylish Contemporary	3,500 Coins	80	240	3.1 days	8 neighbors	3 x 3
Apartment Complex	4,500 Coins	90	210	1 day	Level 15 or 15 City Cash	4 x 4
Ranch House	6,000 Coins	100	189	18 hours	10 neighbors	4 x 4
TV Terrace	10,500 Coins	190	11	5 minutes	Retail goals at Level 13	4 x 4
Milan Apartments	7,000 Coins	100	215	1 day	Level 23 or 23 City Cash	4 x 4
Upscale Condos	8,000 Coins	110	52	1 hour	Level 25 or 25 City Cash	4 x 4
Bay Point Duplex	30,000 Coins	230	102	4 hours	Level 27 or 27 City Cash	4 x 4
Tuscan Villa	9,500 Coins	110	80	2 hours	Level 29 or 29 City Cash	3 x 3
Colonial Chalet	10,000 Coins	120	158	8 hours	15 neighbors	3 x 3
Hotel Suites	12,500 Coins	130	231	2.1 days	Level 35 or 35 City Cash	3 x 6
Sprawling Mansion	15,000 Coins	140	195	18 hours	Level 40 or 40 City Cash	3 x 6
Skyscraper Condos	500,000 Coins	150	105	4 hours	None	4 x 4
Courtyard House	45 City Cash	150	105	4 hours	None	5 x 5
Midtown Apartments	1,100,000 Coins	310	84	2 hours	Level 53 or 53 City Cash	4 x 4

(continued)

Table 4-1 *(continued)*

Name	Cost	Population	Rent	Collection Time	Requirements	Size
Glass Condos	600,000 Coins	160	165	8 hours	Level 55 or 55 City Cash	4 x 4
Atrium Lofts	750,000 Coins	170	220	1 day	Level 60 or 60 City Cash	5 x 5
Newlywed House	N/A	100	13	5 minutes	Wedding Collection	3 x 3
Penthouse Tower	N/A	220	230	1 day	Daily Raffle Prize	3 x 3
Parkside Villa	1,750,000 Coins	350	12	5 minutes	Level 63 or 63 City Cash	4 x 4

Earning Money with Businesses

Face it: There's very little you can do nowadays that doesn't cost money. It's the same thing in CityVille.

Using businesses to increase your cash flow is a necessity. In fact, it's the number one method for raising the funds you need to build, run, and expand your city. Chapter 5 goes into detail on how to build your businesses, and Chapter 9 gets into more detail about how to use businesses to turn your one-stoplight town into a budding metropolis.

Every city starts with two businesses: a Bakery and a Flower Kiosk. The first time you place and build a new business, you're given the opportunity to name it, as shown in Figure 4-3. Get creative! Each subsequent business of that type that you build has that name as well, so be sure it's something that you like.

If your business' name is offensive or vulgar in any way, Zynga may remove it. Also, be sure to choose the name wisely because whenever you place a franchise in a neighbor's city, it has that name! See Chapter 6 for more on building franchise stores in neighboring cities.

To get started building your businesses, click the Businesses tab in the Build menu to display a listing of all the available businesses you can build in your city, as shown in Figure 4-4. Each listing shows a picture of the business and how much it costs. If you hover your mouse over the image, you see the following information:

  ✔ How many Goods are required to supply the business

  ✔ How much money the business earns

Figure 4-3: Naming your new business.

 A business' profits can be increased from the listed baseline when decorations are placed around them. See the next section for more on using decorations.

Figure 4-4: Select your businesses.

Zynga frequently adds new business options to the game, but Table 4-2 shows the business available for purchase as of this writing.

Table 4-2		Businesses Available			
Name	**Cost**	**Earnings**	**Supply**	**Size**	**Requirements**
Empty Lot	0 Coins	Varies	Varies	4 x 4	None
Bakery	200 Coins	40 Coins	10 Goods	3 x 3	None
Flower Kiosk	400 Coins	95 Coins	25 Goods	3 x 3	None
Coffee Shop	600 Coins	320 Coins	100 Goods	3 x 3	Population 50 or 3 Cash
Toy Store	800 Coins	180 Coins	50 Goods	3 x 3	Population 100 or 4 Cash
Burger Joint	1,000 Coins	240 Coins	75 Goods	3 x 3	Population 150 or 5 Cash
Video Game Store	1,300 Coins	50 Coins	10 Goods	3 x 3	8 neighbors
Diner	1,600 Coins	230 Coins	50 Goods	3 x 3	Population 350 or 7 Cash
Cosmetic Store	1,900 Coins	120 Coins	25 Goods	3 x 3	Population 400 or 8 Cash
Pool Hall	2,200 Coins	420 Coins	100 Goods	4 x 4	Population 500 or 9 Cash
Bike Shop	2,500 Coins	330 Coins	75 Goods	3 x 3	9 neighbors
Bookstore	3,000 Coins	430 Coins	100 Goods	3 x 3	Goal completion
Seasonal Clothing	20 City Cash	368 Coins	80 Goods	3 x 3	None
Hot Cocoa Shop	15 City Cash	441 Coins	100 Goods	3 x 3	None
Shoe Store	3,500 Coins	572 Coins	130 Goods	3 x 3	Population 700 or 12 Cash
Noodle Shop	4,000 Coins	405 Coins	90 Goods	3 x 3	15 Cash
City Dojo	4,250 Coins	495 Coins	110 Goods	3 x 3	Population 750 or 12 Cash
French Restaurant	4,500 Coins	495 Coins	110 Goods	3 x 3	Goal completion
Laundromat	5,000 Coins	515 Coins	115 Goods	3 x 3	Population 1,000 or 17 Cash
Tofu Burger	5,000 Coins	507 Coins	115 Goods	3 x 3	Population 1,100 or 17 Cash
Sunglasses Store	5,500 Coins	534 Coins	120 Goods	3 x 3	Population 1,200 or 18 Cash

Name	Cost	Earnings	Supply	Size	Requirements
Department Store	8,000 Coins	588 Coins	135 Goods	4 x 4	Goal completion
City Supermarket	5,750 Coins	569 Coins	130 Goods	4 x 4	Population 1250 or 21 Cash
Italian Restaurant	6,500 Coins	645 Coins	150 Goods	3 x 3	Population 1,500 or 40 Cash
Appliance Store	25 City Cash	405 Coins	90 Goods	3 x 3	None
Seafood Restaurant	7,500 Coins	609 Coins	140 Goods	3 x 3	15 neighbors
Handbag Store	10,000 Coins	654 Coins	120 Goods	3 x 3	Population 2,000 or 30 Cash
Sushi Bar	12,500 Coins	605 Coins	110 Goods	3 x 3	Population 2,300 or 35 Cash
Wedding Store	15,000 Coins	702 Coins	130 Goods	3 x 3	Population 2,750 or 40 Cash
Cinema	100.000 Coins	749 Coins	140 Goods	4 x 4	Goal completion
Chic Boutique	250,000 Coins	795 Coins	150 Goods	3 x 3	Level 55 or 50 Cash
Jewelry Store	500,000 Coins	830 Coins	155 Goods	3 x 3	Level 60 or 55 Cash
Furniture Store	750,000 Coins	864 Coins	160 Goods	3 x 3	Population 8,000 or 65 Cash
Music Store	900,000 Coins	881 Coins	163 Goods	3 x 3	Population 9,000 or 75 Cash
Tower Eats	1,000,000 Coins	900 Coins	165 Goods	4 x 4	None
Corner Store	Pea Collection	270 Coins	60 Goods	3 x 3	None
Tavern	Downtown Collection	352 Coins	80 Goods	3 x 3	None
Tuxedo Rental	Jetsetter Collection	575 Coins	125 Goods	3 x 3	None

* Stores that were only available through expired holiday promotions are not included in this table.

The Corner Store, Tavern, and Tuxedo Rental buildings can't be purchased with Coins or City Cash. Each requires you to redeem collections and then place the building from your inventory.

Increasing Payouts with Decorations

Click the Decorations tab in the Build menu to see a list of all the decorations you can purchase for your city, as shown in Figure 4-5. The purchase price is listed below the item. When you hover your mouse over each item's button, you see the following information:

- ✔ The name of the decoration
- ✔ The percentage the decoration will increase payouts by, if any

Figure 4-5: The Decorations tab of the Build menu.

Most decorations carry a bonus with them that increases the payout of nearby buildings by a certain percentage. These decorations provide their bonus to all houses and businesses within a three-square radius of their position. This bonus area is shown as a green outline when placing the decoration, and affected buildings are highlighted with a Bonus message as you decide on your placement position, as shown in Figure 4-6.

For example, if you place Park Plaza (which provides a 10-percent bonus) near Modern Chateau (which produces rent of 200 Coins), you receive 220 Coins in rent every time you collect from the Chateau.

One building can get bonuses from multiple nearby decorations, though these stacking bonuses apply only to the base production from that building (so the bonus portion from one decoration is not itself further increased from further decorations). Chapter 9 discusses the best ways to utilize decorations in your city.

Figure 4-6: Placing decorations can increase payouts.

Not all decorations give bonus payouts. Hover your mouse over the decoration you're interested in purchasing to confirm the size of the bonus before purchasing.

Some decorations are locked until you reach certain levels, have the right amount of neighbors, or complete various goals. Others, such as the Penguin or White Bunny, can be acquired only as a gift. There are also many seasonal and holiday decorations available for purchase. For example, as this book was written, there were many winter-themed decorations, including an Ice Rink and a Ski Slope. There were also decorations for Valentine's Day and the Chinese New Year celebration.

Decorations are the perfect way to make your city look exactly the way you want. Some people get really creative and create elaborate gardens to make their city beautiful. Others pile up the high bonus-paying decorations around to increase the payout of their buildings considerably. Figure 4-6 shows how using just one decoration, the Arboretum (16 percent), can grow your profits while also beautifying your city. Go ahead and have some fun. Your city is your canvas!

If you only have one decoration with a higher payout, such as the 64-percent bonus-granting Tennis Court, consider moving it around your city to be close to each building before each building collection. Although this process requires lots of time and free space around your buildings, it's a great way to collect a lot of City Coins quickly. Remember, there are no rules saying a decoration has to be static!

The decorations in Table 4-3 are part of the permanent decorations collection. Zynga regularly releases holiday and season-themed decorations that change frequently. Always check the Specials tab of the Build menu, which we discuss in the section "Keeping Track of New Items," later in this chapter.

Table 4-3		Available Decorations		
Decoration	**Cost**	**Size**	**Bonus (%)**	**Requirement**
Asphalt Road	10 Coins	3 x 3	0	None
City Sidewalk	20 Coins	1 x 1	0	None
Parking Lot	10 Coins	3 x 3	0	None
St Bernard	5 Cash	1 x 1	0	None
Rocket Babysitter	200 Coins	1 x 1	1	None
Happy Shoppers	25 Cash	3 x 3	18	None
Bounce Castle	30 Cash	3 x 3	18	None
City Flag	50 Coins	1 x 1	1	None
Flower Patch	50 Coins	1 x 1	1	None
Blue Flowers	75 Coins	1 x 1	1	None
Pot of Flowers	100 Coins	1 x 1	1	None
Pink Flowers	300 Coins	2 x 2	4	None
Shade Tree	50 Coins	1 x 1	1	None
Fall Tree	2 Cash	1 x 1	1	None
Arboretum	4,000 Coins	4 x 4	16	None
Lion Bush Sculpture	10 Cash	2 x 2	8	None
Stop Sign	100 Coins	1 x 1	1	A Park (see Chapter 8)
Lamp Post	75 Coins	1 x 1	1	None
Brick Wall	50 Coins	1 x 1	1	None
Sturdy Fence	75 Coins	1 x 1	1	None

Decoration	Cost	Size	Bonus (%)	Requirement
Barricade	200 Coins	2 x 2	4	None
Picnic Table	75 Coins	1 x 1	1	None
Snack Cart	100 Coins	1 x 1	1	None
Blue Dog House	50 Coins	1 x 1	1	None
Brown Cow	200 Coins	1 x 1	1	None
Ole Windmill	7 Cash	1 x 1	2	None
Bronze Statue	3,000 Coins	2 x 1	2	None
Ornate Fountain	15 Cash	3 x 3	18	None
Marble Arches	20 Cash	4 x 2	16	None
Red Lighthouse	15,000 Coins	3 x 3	11	Captain Rusty World Tour (see Chapter 8)
Romantic Gazebo	15 Cash	3 x 3	18	None
Rocky Hill	24,000 Coins	4 x 4	20	15 neighbors
Tiered Fountain	15 Cash	3 x 3	18	None
Swing Set Playground	13,500 Coins	3 x 3	11	A Grade School (see Chapter 8)
Bridge Pond	15 Cash Coins	4 x 4	32	None
Park Plaza	13,500 Coins	3 x 3	10	A Park (see Chapter 8)
Bandstand	15 Cash	4 x 4	32	None
Expo Tent	9,000 Coins	3 x 2	7	The State Fair (see Chapter 8)
Swimming Pool	25 Cash	4 x 4	32	None
Batting Cage	12,000 Coins	4 x 2	9	Preparing city to become the Capital (see Chapter 8)

(continued)

Table 4-3 *(continued)*				
Decoration	*Cost*	*Size*	*Bonus (%)*	*Requirement*
Basketball Court	25 Cash	4 x 4	32	None
Tennis Court	35 Cash	8 x 4	64	None
Spring Gazebo	15,000 Coins	3 x 3	1	Wedding Pavilion quest (see Chapter 8)
Wedding Pavilion	60,000 Coins	4 x 4	17	Groomsman's Links quest (see Chapter 8)
Highway Billboard	N/A	3 x 3	9	Silver Screen collection (see Chapter 3)
Street Clock	Gift	1 x 1	1	None
Racing Ride	Gift	1 x 1	1	None
Winter Oak	Gift	1 x 1	1	None
Orange Flowers	Gift	1 x 1	1	None
Plaza Flowers	Gift	1 x 1	1	None
Fence	Gift	1 x 1	1	None
White Cow	Gift	1 x 1	1	Level 15
Poinciana Tree	Gift	2 x 2	4	Level 15
Horse	Gift	1 x 1	1	Level 20
Hanging Flower	Gift	1 x 1	1	Level 20
Moose	Gift	1 x 1	1	Level 20
Willow Tree	Gift	2 x 2	4	Level 30
Fountain	Gift	3 x 3	9	Level 40
Pig	Gift	1 x 1	1	7 neighbors
White Bunny	Gift	1 x 1	1	10 neighbors
Penguin	Gift	1 x 1	0	15 neighbors

Growing and Storing Goods with Farming

Click the Farming tab in the Build menu to see a list of all the seeds you can purchase for your city, as well as the option to create an empty farm plot, as shown in Figure 4-7. See Chapter 5 for more information on planting crops.

In addition to seeds, this menu is where you purchase storage buildings to collect ever-important Goods to supply your businesses. To find these options, just click the right arrow all the way to the end of the menu.

Figure 4-7: The Farming tab of the Build menu.

The price of each item is listed below the item and, in the case of seeds, those prices are for one seeded plot. When you hover your mouse over the picture, you see the following information:

- The name of the seed or storage building
- How many Goods each seeded plot will produce, or in the case of storage buildings, how many Goods it will hold
- The time required between harvests for seeds

As you can see in Table 4-4, there are ten crops available for purchase, as of this writing. Nine of them are bought with City Coins, and one seasonal-themed option can be purchased with 5 City Cash. Though spending so much Cash on a single crop may seem excessive, these crops come with the upside of growing instantly. If you're in desperate need for some Goods and have some City Cash to spare, this may be a good option to consider.

Table 4-4		Seeds		
Crop	*Cost (Coins)*	*Harvest Time*	*Goods*	*Requirement*
Strawberries	20	5 min	15	None
Carrot	16	8 hours	70	None
Seasonal-themed	5 City Cash	Instant growth	115	None
Corn	62	1 day	110	Level 4 or 4 City Cash
Eggplant	28	1 hour	30	Level 6 or 6 City Cash

(continued)

Table 4-4 *(continued)*

Crop	Cost (Coins)	Harvest Time	Goods	Requirement
Watermelon	36	4 hours	45	Level 9 or 9 City Cash
Cabbage	64	1.6 days	114	Level 10 or 10 City Cash
Cranberries	49	12 hours	80	Level 12 or 12 City Cash
Pumpkin	52	18 hours	90	Level 15 or 15 City Cash
Wheat	71	2.1 days	130	Level 20 or 20 City Cash
Peas	85	3.1 days	155	Level 25 or 25 City Cash

Four storage buildings are available, as shown in Table 4-5. Three of the buildings are purchased with City Coins, and the remaining one is with City Cash. The more the building costs, the more Goods it holds. Every city starts with the Red Barn, which holds 415 Goods. You can have any number of storage buildings in your city, and they don't have to be placed next to roads. Because of this, we recommend having as many as you can fit so you always have Goods on hand.

Table 4-5   Storage Buildings

Storage	Cost (Coins)	Goods Held	Requirement	Size
Silo	250	100	None	2 x 2
Red Barn*	1,000	415	Level 8 or 8 City Cash	4 x 4
Sticks	1,125	485	Level 12 or 12 City Cash	3 x 6
Cargo Shed	20 City Cash	1,000	None	3 x 3

Each city comes populated with one Red Barn. This is for each additional barn.

The longer the seed germination time, the more expensive it is and the more Goods it produces. Consider staggering your planting times and crop types to ensure you always have some Goods at your disposal. See Chapter 9 for more information on efficient farming.

Utilizing Shipping to Collect Goods

Click the Shipping tab in the Build menu to display a list of shipping missions, as well as the pier and boat items that are necessary to perform such missions. The price for each selection is below the item, and if you hover your mouse over the item's button, you see the following information:

- ✔ The name of the item
- ✔ In the case of missions, the number of Goods the mission provides
- ✔ How long the mission lasts

After you complete the New Seaport goal (see Chapter 8), you can buy piers and boats for your city. These boats let you perform shipping missions as another method of collecting Goods.

Piers can be placed only on the coastline, as shown in Figure 4-8. This means that most of their massive size extends into otherwise useless water, making them more efficient than they first seem based on space. Depending on the shape of the coast and the precise placement of the pier, you may use anywhere from 0 to 16 usable plots of land in its placement.

Figure 4-8: A coastline populated with a couple of piers.

Although the Boat House has to exist inside the area of your land expansion, the actual pier can extend into darker water that isn't technically part of your city.

Here are the two schools of thought regarding optimum placement of piers and boats.

✔ **Jam piers as close to each other as possible.** This method, as shown in Figure 4-9, maximizes the storage-per-land use, but you may not be able to keep as many boats because some of the boat positions overlap.

Figure 4-9: It's a tight squeeze.

✔ **Spread piers apart so that each pier can have as many as eight boats along its docks.** This method, refer to Figure 4-8, maximizes the opportunity to have simultaneous shipping missions going on but can lead to slightly inefficient use of your coastline.

Play around and see which you prefer, but be careful: You can't move a pier unless you first remove all the boats attached to it.

To schedule a shipping mission, you first need to buy a pier and at least one boat. Then follow these steps.

1. **Click the Build menu and then click the Shipping tab.**

   The Shipping tab, as shown in Figure 4-10, appears. You can also click an empty ship to bring up the tab. Click the left and right arrows to see more options. Hover your mouse over any option to see that mission's name, its return in Goods, and the amount of time it will take to for the ships to return to the pier with goods. This information is also contained in Table 4-6.

2. **Click the shipping mission you want to undertake.**

   If you got to the Shipping tab through the Build menu, you have to click a boat to use for the mission. The ship sails off into the ocean, leaving a pale outline and a buoy in its place.

Figure 4-10: The Shipping tab.

You can click further boats to send them all on the mission you've just chosen. If you want to select a different mission for another boat, you have to click the red circle with a slash through it in the Tools menu in the bottom-right corner of the play area.

3. Wait for the boat to return with Goods; then click it to unload them.

Goods icons fall out of the boat. You can click these icons to collect them, as normal. Unloading a ship takes 1 Energy from your meter.

Table 4-6	Shipping Options on the Build Menu		
Location	Cost (Coins)	Shipping Time	Goods
Pier	5,000	N/A	N/A
Boat	100	N/A	N/A
San Francisco	25	5 minutes	19
Sydney	70	8 hours	87
Paris	95	1 day	137
Shanghai	44	1 hour	38
London	55	4 hours	56
Dubai	76	12 hours	100
New York	79	18 hours	112
Rio	109	2.1 days	162
Rome	131	3.1 days	194
Caribbean	101	1.6 days	146

Raising Your Population Cap with Community Buildings

Click the Community Buildings tab in the Build menu to see a selection of different municipal buildings, as shown in Figure 4-11. Placing these buildings in your city raises your *population cap* — the maximum number of residents your city can have. This number is the one to the right of the slash and is found below your city's name at the top of your neighbor bar.

Figure 4-11: The Community Buildings tab of the Build menu.

As with the categories in the Build menu, each Community Building shows the purchase price below the item. If you hover your mouse over the building's button, you see the name of the building and the number of residents that building allows. This number represents how much your population cap will increase when the building is placed.

Each Community Building can be collected every 23 hours for a profit of 250 City Coins and either 1 or 2 Energy and Experience Points (XP). The precise amount of Energy and XP you receive is random with each collection — sometimes you luck out and get two of each, sometimes you get less.

Fulfilling requirements for community buildings

In Chapter 6, we discuss the importance of having neighbors to rely on throughout the game. This includes the need for neighbors to "work" in your community buildings. You read that right! For many of the community buildings, you have to ask your neighbors to join the crew in order to open the buildings and take advantage of the extra population they allow. If that's not a reason to have a lot of neighbors, we don't know what is. Even if you have a lot of neighbors, that doesn't guarantee that they'll accept your help request. This is one of the reasons why building community buildings can sometimes be a time-consuming process.

Even if a particular Community Building doesn't require help from your neighbors, it will require you to collect sets of different construction materials that you can't purchase directly through the Build menu. These items can be gifted to you by neighbors, as we discuss in more detail in Chapter 6 or you have the option to purchase them using City Cash after you place the building's frame into your city. The materials are

- ✔ Marble
- ✔ A city seal
- ✔ A building grant
- ✔ Gold plating
- ✔ Ribbon

Table 4-7 shows you which community buildings need a staff of neighbors and which need gifted materials in order to complete. *Note:* No Community Building currently requires both staff and materials to open.

Table 4-7	Community Buildings					
Name	*Cost (Coins)*	*Population Allowance*	*Staff*	*Materials*	*Goal/Level*	*Size*
City Hall	1,000	50	3	0	Plant a flag	4 x 4
Post Office	1,000	50	5	0	Level 4 or 4 City Cash	4 x 4
Wedding Hall	1,250	70	6	0	Level 5 or 5 City Cash	3 x 3
Police	2,000	100	7	0	Level 7 or 7 City Cash	3 x 3
Emergency Clinic	4,000	200	10	0	Level 10 or 10 City Cash	4 x 4
Bank	6,000	250	10	0	Level 13 or 13 City Cash	4 x 4
Museum	8,000	300	0	1	Level 15 or 15 City Cash	4 x 4

(continued)

Table 4-7 (continued)

Name	Cost (Coins)	Population Allowance	Staff	Materials	Goal/Level	Size
Television Tower	12,000	350	7	0	Level 17 or 17 City Cash	4 x 4
Library	16,000	400	10	0	Level 20 or 20 City Cash	4 x 4
Zynga Gazette	18,000	450	10	0	Level 23 or 23 City Cash	4 x 4
Grade School	20,000	500	0	3	Increase population	4 x 4
Carousel	25,000	700	0	4	Bring State Fair to town	3 x 3
Middle School	27,500	800	12	0	Level 32 or 32 City Cash	4 x 4
Firehouse	30,000	900	0	5	Population 4,000 or 35 City Cash	6 x 3
High School	35,000	1,100	0	6	Level 40 or 40 City Cash	6 x 6
Hospital	40,000	1,300	0	7	Level 45 or 5 City Cash	8 x 4
Baseball Field	50,000	1,500	0	8	Feed the fans	6 x 6
Court House	100,000	1,700	0	9	Level 55 or 55 City Cash	4 x 4
Modern Art Gallery	200,000	1,900	12	0	Level 60 or 60 City Cash	5 x 5

Name	Cost (Coins)	Population Allowance	Staff	Materials	Goal/Level	Size
Observatory	200,000	1,900	12	0	Level 65 or 65 City Cash	4 x 4
Visitor's Center	Zynga provided	230	4	0	Level 15	4 x 4
Mint	Goal completion	1,000	10	0	Collect 1 million City Coins	6 x 4
Capitol Building	Goal completion	1,000	10	0	Build a Hospital and collect from it three times	5 x 5
Clerk's Office	Zynga provided	0	0	5	None	4 x 4

Be sure to accept any staffing or gift requests from your neighbors that appear in your CityVille Messages tab (which we discuss in Chapter 3). Providing this help costs you nothing more than a click and can increase goodwill from your neighbors significantly. Remember, your neighbors are doing exactly what you're trying to do — building community buildings so they can increase the population of their cities!

Getting more use out of community buildings

Gone are the days where community buildings only raise your population cap. Now the Clerk's Office and Visitor's Center buildings allow you to have more control over your city as well as information on its statistics, such as the value of your city in Coins.

Clerk's Office

Zynga made it easy for you to see which neighbors are actively helping with your city by developing the Clerk's Office. This building is provided by Zynga to all players free of charge and can be found in your inventory.

Like many other community buildings, this building requires three sets of construction materials to complete; however, these materials are different from those we mention earlier in the "Fulfilling requirements for community buildings" section. To complete the Clerk's Office, you need to receive the following items as gifts from your neighbors or purchase them using City Cash:

- An ink pad
- A city seal
- Marble
- A manila folder
- A visor

Now for the best part. The purpose of the Clerk's Office is to give you the ability to change not only the name of your city, but also the names of your businesses.

Before you try to rename all 100 or so of your businesses, there's a catch. For each business that you want to rename, you need at least three signatures from your neighbors saying they agree to the name change. If you have a business with franchises in neighboring cities, you have to get extra signatures because the name change affects their cityscape as well.

Visitor's Center

The Visitor's Center is another Zynga-provided Community Building that requires four of your neighbors to be staff members in order to open.

Clicking the Visitor's Center in yours — or any of your neighbor's — cities shows you the top ten visitors who stop by and lend a hand as well as interesting facts, such as how much the city is worth in Coins, the total number of residences and businesses, and whether any franchise plots are available. Although much of the information provided isn't particularly useful in game play, it's always interesting to see how your city stacks up against another's. Who knows? You may see that a neighbor's city is worth twice as much as yours, but they may have more trees, which carry a 1-percent bonus payout. A little strategy, anyone?

Whenever you help in a neighbor's city, be sure to check out its Visitor's Center to see whether it has any available franchise lots. Sometimes the city is so densely packed that it may be difficult to see them.

Doing More with Energy and Expansions

Energy and land expansions go hand in hand in your virtual city. Without Energy, you can't build or collect from homes and businesses to earn money; and without money, you can't expand your city; and without expanding your city, you can't grow your wallet even more . . . Do you see where we're going with this? If you want to be successful in CityVille, you have to purchase land expansions and have enough Energy to perform important daily tasks in your city to reap your profits.

Energy

Click the Energy tab in the Build menu to display a selection of Energy Batteries available for purchase, as shown in Figure 4-12. Energy Batteries reside in your inventory until you're ready to use them and provide a one-time Energy point boost. Energy Batteries can be purchased only with City Cash. You can read more about acquiring and utilizing City Cash in Chapter 7.

Figure 4-12: The Energy tab of the Build menu.

Energy points are arguably the most valuable commodities in CityVille. You need Energy to perform tasks, such as collecting Coins from homes and businesses, building buildings, harvesting crops, and collecting Goods from boats. In other words, in CityVille, Energy makes the world go 'round, and you won't get very far without it!

As of this writing, you can purchase only three sizes of Energy Batteries from the Build menu. The more you buy, the more you save — that is, spending more City Cash gets you a better rate of Energy return on your purchase. Here are the Energy Battery options available to you through the Build menu:

- ✔ 3 Energy points cost 3 City Cash
- ✔ 7 Energy points cost 6 City Cash
- ✔ 12 Energy points cost 9 City Cash

Land expansions

You can view available land expansions by clicking the Expansions tab in the Build menu, as shown in Figure 4-13. Purchasing a land expansion lets you add a 12-x-12 block of developable land to the border of your city, giving you more space to place buildings and decorations.

Figure 4-13: Expanding your city limits.

TIP

After you place an expansion, you most likely have to chop down trees to clear the area for development. Each group of trees you chop down costs 1 Energy, and if you're clearing a lot of space, that can add up quickly. If you aren't in a hurry to start building right away, consider leaving your trees for a neighbor to cut down when he stops by for a visit. You can also send your neighbor a Facebook message asking them to help you out.

You can purchase a land expansion at any level, as long as you have enough City Coins and building permits. These building permits are usually the biggest obstacle to your expansion because you can get them only as gifts from neighbors, as we discuss in Chapter 6. The number of building permits needed for an expansion increases with each expansion you purchase. For example, your first expansion requires only one building permit to purchase, but if you've expanded seven times before, you need eight building permits to expand an eighth time. Table 4-8 shows you how many City Coins and building permits you need to spend each time you want to expand your city. As of this writing, each expansion after the 27th costs 500,000 City Coins and requires 100 permits. You can have a maximum of 40 expansions.

Table 4-8	Land Expansions	
Expansion Number	*Cost (Coins)*	*Permits Required*
1	20,000	1
2	21,000	2
3	22,000	3
4	23,000	4
5	25,000	5
6	28,000	6
7	32,000	7

Expansion Number	Cost (Coins)	Permits Required
8	37,000	8
9	43,000	9
10	50,000	10
11	60,000	12
12	75,000	15
13	95,000	16
14	120,000	18
15	150,000	20
16	185,000	24
17	225,000	28
18	270,000	32
19	320,000	40
20	375,000	45
21	435,000	50
22	500,000	55
23	500,000	60
24	500,000	70
25	500,000	80
26	500,000	90
27	500,000	100

TIP

Land is a valuable commodity in CityVille, so it's important to make use of every inch of it. Unless you're interested in building a pier, you shouldn't place your expansions over the top of shorelines or waterways that can't be used for buildings, decorations, and crops.

Distinguishing Your City with Landmarks and Wonders

Click the Landmarks tab in the Build menu to purchase famous landmarks to add to your city. These buildings act like community buildings, raising your population cap by 2,000, but give a much larger 1,000 Coin payout every 23 hours. More than that though, these massive buildings help set your city apart from your neighbors who only have tiny houses and shops. It's no wonder that these buildings carry a hefty price tag — 2 million City Coins!

Table 4-9 shows you the landmarks that are currently available and all the information pertaining to them.

Table 4-9		Landmarks	
Landmark	*Cost (Coins)*	*Requirements*	*Staff*
Pearl Tower	2,000,000	None	12
Big Ben	2,000,000	Population 5,000 or 35 City Cash	12
Chicago Tower	2,000,000	Population 7,000 or 40 City Cash	12
Empire State Building	2,000,000	Population 10,000 or 50 City Cash	12

Clicking the Wonders tab, the last one in the Build menu, shows you nothing, as of this writing! As shown in Figure 4-14, a teaser Coming Soon! message is in place of items you can purchase. One can only speculate what these items will be, but knowing Zynga, they're going to be great additions to your city. Hey, yet another reason why you should come back to CityVille to play!

Figure 4-14: Wonders coming soon!

Keeping Track of New Items

We've saved the best (and first) for last. Clicking the first tab in the Build menu brings up Specials, such as the ones in Figure 4-15. This is the place where you can spruce up your city with seasonal and holiday-themed items including decorations, crops, and buildings. Check this section often because Zynga adds new items frequently.

Figure 4-15: The Specials tab of the Build menu.

In Chapter 6, we talk about keeping up with the Joneses, and purchasing new items from the Specials menu is a great way to not only keep up with them, but if you're lucky, you'll beat *them* to it! Who doesn't want to be the Joneses that everyone else has to keep up with?

Some of the items in the Specials tab require you to complete goals in order to purchase them. For more information on goals, see Chapter 8. Others may require you to be on a certain level of the game. The rules for the items in the Specials tab are the same; decorations have bonus payouts, crops have ripening times, and buildings generate revenue.

Because these items are seasonal, they're available only for a limited time. When you see something you like, make sure you buy it as soon as you can because the items remain in your city forever — or as long as you want them to. Don't let the clock run out!

Starting Your City Right

In This Chapter

▶ Erecting buildings

▶ Planting crops

▶ Understanding the profit collection cycle

▶ Getting tips for new city managers

*A*fter you set up your Facebook account and install the game, you're ready to get started building your soon-to-be booming metropolis. If you haven't done either of those things, head to Chapter 2 to find out how. Don't worry; we'll wait for you.

The first sections of this chapter help you get the lay of the land. We walk you through what you see when you start the game and where you should go from there. Next, we get into a couple of firsts, such as erecting your first buildings and planting your first crops before getting into the rent collection cycle. Finally, we present a few quick tips that get you on the road to being a successful new city manager!

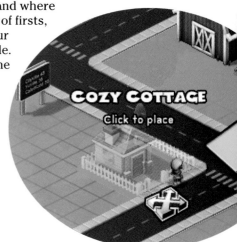

Surveying Your Base City: Level 1

Every CityVille player starts with the following statistics and in-game currency:

┃ ✓ **Level:** 1

┃ ✓ **Experience Points (XP):** 0

┃ ✓ **Coins:** 7,000

- ✔ **City Cash:** 5
- ✔ **Energy:** 12
- ✔ **Goods:** 100
- ✔ **Plowed and planted land:** Four plots with strawberries
- ✔ **Houses:** One
- ✔ **Storage:** One barn, which stores up to 715 Goods
- ✔ **Franchise plots:** One

The game starts with a short, interactive tutorial in which your guide Samantha instructs you on the city-building process, as shown in Figure 5-1.

Figure 5-1: Let the tutorial begin!

You have to participate in the tutorial but don't worry; it's easy and takes very little time. The tutorial gives you a crash course in doing the basics, such as placing buildings (as shown in Figure 5-2) and completing goals (as shown in Figure 5-3). We get into those things in more detail later in this chapter, so if you forget what you found out in the tutorial, you can come back to the following sections of the book and dive right back in.

Figure 5-2: Samantha shows you how to place your first home.

Figure 5-3: Don't forget about the goals!

This tutorial is important for many reasons — namely, because it's when you name your city, so choose wisely! After you settle on a name, it appears at the top left of your neighbor bar. (For more information on changing your city's name, see Chapter 11.)

After you choose your city name, you're introduced via a newspaper head-line to your first major goal of the game — becoming Mayor of your city. Becoming Mayor is no easy task and requires you to complete many goals along the way. Chapter 8 talks more about completing goals and the path to mayorship.

Samantha pops up every now and again when something new is introduced to the game, such as a new goal or new features. Plus, you're in luck: She's your very first neighbor!

Erecting your first buildings

Buildings, whether dwellings or stores, are the heart and soul of CityVille. After all, have you ever head of a city without buildings? The quick tutorial that the game starts with shows you how to place your first residence, the Cozy Cottage (but in case you missed it, see the steps later in this section). The Cozy Cottage is one of the smallest buildings in CityVille, costs 200 Coins, and increases your population by 10, which means it holds the fewest amount of residents out of any of the other homes.

Other types of buildings available to you this early in the game are busi-nesses and storage buildings, such as the Red Barn, which is one of the build-ings that already populates your city. Chances are at this early stage in the game, you don't yet need to increase your storage capabilities; however, we discuss them in more detail in Chapter 4.

To place a building in your city, follow these steps:

1. **From the Build menu at the bottom of your screen, choose the build-ing you want to build.**

   We discuss the different types of buildings in Chapter 4. After you com-plete the tutorial mentioned earlier, you are allowed to place only the Cozy Cottage in your new city. After you finish the tutorial, you can purchase three types of homes with City Coins: the Cozy Cottage, the Family Townhouse, and the Skyscraper Condos. You can also purchase one home — the Lake House — with City Cash. You also can build two buildings: a Bakery and a Flower Kiosk. Whichever option you choose, the steps to build them are the same.

TIP

When deciding on which homes to build first, take into consideration how much time you'll spend playing the game. For example, the Cozy Cottage gives you rent of 50 Coins every hour, and the Family Townhouse nets you 100 Coins every four hours. If you'll work in your city every hour to collect from your Cozy Cottage, you'll collect 200 Coins in those same four hours. However, if you won't be returning to your city that frequently, you'd be better off starting off with the Family Townhouse to collect more Coins each time (For more on choosing which homes are the best for your city, see Chapter 9.)

2. **With the building you choose, hover your mouse over a plot of land to find an empty space in your city to place it.**

   When you hover over a plot of land, a green, yellow, or red square appears. The *green* square, as shown in Figure 5-4, means you can place the building; *yellow* means you can place the building, but residents won't move in and you won't.

3. **Place the building onto the plot of land.**

   Click the plot of land you selected, and the frame of your building is set down.

   Now that you have your frame, you have to expend Energy to build the building by clicking the frame. The amount of Energy you have to spend depends on the particular building; it ranges from 2 to 8 Energy points. (For more information on where to acquire Energy, see Chapter 7.)

Figure 5-4: You have the green light to place your building.

If you built a house, a moving van parks in front of the house and your new residents get out, cheering with excitement at their new home! If you built a business, you have to click it to supply it with Goods. Then, your business opens to a flourish of balloons flying and cheering residents.

If you construct a business and don't have enough Goods to supply the business the first time, your business won't open until you do. Be sure to be well-stocked with Goods before you build businesses by harvesting the strawberry crops your city starts with or planting new crops, as discussed in the following section.

Planting your first crops

When you start out in your city, the only way you can gain Goods to supply your businesses is by growing them. You start the game with four farm plots planted with strawberries, the cheapest and fastest-growing crop you can purchase with City Coins in CityVille. You can purchase a plot of strawberries for 20 City Coins, and they're ready to harvest in just 5 minutes!

If you want, you can purchase a seasonal crop that Zynga changes occasionally. All these seasonal crops grow instantly and provide you with 115 Goods. The catch? Each plot costs a certain amount of City Cash, which is acquired either by gaining levels in the game or by purchasing with real-life money. The cost of these crops varies, but they typically start at 3 City Cash per farm plot.

We discuss all the farming options available to you in detail in Chapter 4, but we start with the basics here — strawberries. Strawberries are the only plants you can purchase with City Coins at this level in the game. You harvest them after 5 minutes and receive 15 Goods per crop. If you have some City Cash burning a hole in your virtual pocket, you can spend it to plant the seasonal crop, which we mention earlier.

Although the four plots you begin with may be sufficient in these first stages of the game, eventually you want to increase the amount of land you use for farming so you can harvest more Goods to supply your stores.

The following steps walk you through how to expand and utilize your farmland in your city:

1. **Choose Build⇨Farming.**

   The Farming menu appears.

2. **Click the Farm Plot button.**

3. Hover your cursor over the spot where you want to place the farm plot and click that square with your mouse.

Each plot takes up one square in your city, they can be placed anywhere, and they don't have to be connected to roads. After you find an appropriate place for your plot of land, a green square appears, as shown in Figure 5-5. A small square of dirt (or a *plot*) that you plow turns a darker brown. Plowing a plot of land costs 100 Coins per plot. You can place as many plots of land as space and your banks allow; however, we recommend leaving room for some buildings and decorations, which are discussed more in Chapters 4 and 8.

Figure 5-5: Placing farming plots.

4. Choose Build⇨Farming again.

The Farming tab appears. Not all seeds are available for purchase at first, but you unlock more as you gain higher levels (as we describe in Chapter 7).

You can also click the red circle with the line through it on your Tools menu, which we discuss in Chapter 3. Then, click the empty plot of land to automatically bring up the Farming tab of the Build menu.

5. **Click the Strawberry button and then click the empty plot of land in your city.**

   When you click the seed's button, the Build menu disappears and the chosen seed shows up next to your cursor. After you plant them in an empty plot, City Coins are deducted from your bank.

   In addition to strawberries and the seasonal crop, there are 8 other crops with costs ranging from 28 to 85 City Coins per plot. Hovering your mouse over any of the seeds brings up a bubble showing their growing time and how many Goods they produce.

   You can repeat this step as many times as you want to seed multiple plowed plots. If you want to plant a different seed when it becomes available in a previously used plot, choose Build and repeat the process.

   Although planting crops does not expend any Energy points, harvesting them costs 1 Energy per plot, no matter what type of crop it is. This is why you need to carefully plan your planting and harvesting schedule. You don't want to be caught without any Goods — or Energy to harvest them! (For more on using your Energy to help with farming efficiency, see Chapter 9.)

6. **Wait for your crops to ripen.**

   The crops in CityVille have harvest times ranging from 1 hour to 3.1 days. You can check on your crop during this ripening time by hovering your mouse over a seeded plot to display how much time is left until you can harvest it.

   If you wait too long to harvest crops after they ripen, they wither into shriveled, brown husks that aren't worth any Goods. If this happens, you have to go back to Step 1 and re-plow that plot of land. The time it takes a ripened crop to wither is the same as the amount of time it takes for that seed to turn in to a ripened crop.

7. **Click a fully ripened crop to harvest it.**

   The Goods are deposited into your storage buildings, and you expend 1 Energy point. Each time you harvest a plot, you receive either 1 or 2 Experience Points (XP) and you may receive a bonus of extra Goods or items for collections. These bonuses happen at random, so make sure you harvest your crops frequently! For more information on collections and earning XP, see Chapter 7.

Figuring out the profit collection cycle

Farming is just one way to keep your city bustling. After you start erecting buildings, you open a whole new world for yourself — income from rent and profits!

The amount of rent you collect and the time frame in which you collect it in depends on that particular residence. For example, the Cozy Cottage nets 50 City Coins every hour, whereas the Sprawling Mansion brings in 195 City Coins every 18 hours, though you can't place the Sprawling Mansion until later in the game.

You can see how many Coins you'll get from rent and how long the collection cycle is by hovering your mouse over the particular building in the Housing tab of the Build menu, as shown in Figure 5-6. (We discuss the Build menu and the Housing tab in more detail in Chapter 4.) After your house is in place, you can see how much time remains until you can collect rent again by hovering your mouse over the home in your city.

Figure 5-6: Seeing the details of each residence in the Build menu.

Another way to acquire Goods is through utilizing piers and shipping, which are discussed more in Chapter 4. This method runs on a collection cycle as well. The shipping time depends on where you send your ships. For example, sending your ships to San Francisco nets you 19 Goods in a mere 5 minutes, whereas sailing all the way to Rome takes 3.1 days but you get 194 Goods out of that trip. You can see how much time is left until your ships dock at the pier by hovering your mouse over the empty boat spaces represented by buoys at your pier.

The situation is slightly different when collecting profits from businesses. Instead of a specific time frame in which you can collect profits from homes, you collect profits from businesses whenever they run out of Goods. This means that businesses that take only a small number of Goods to run, such as Bakeries, which use 10 Goods, run out of Goods faster than a building, such as the Crab Shack, which takes 140 Goods. (Chapter 9 discusses how to get the right mix of businesses and residences to maximize your profits and Energy usage during the collection cycle.)

Tips for New Managers

Although your new city might not look so hot compared to your veteran CityVille neighbors, don't let these humble beginnings get you down. You, too, can become a CityVille Mayor in a very short time if you stick to the following tips for new managers.

Utilize sidewalks

Roads are one of the biggest wastes of space in CityVille. Don't get us wrong; you need roads to open businesses and build homes. But did you know that your buildings don't need to be *directly* on the road?

A great way to utilize the space behind a current row of buildings is to build a pathway from the road to the back side of your property. Sidewalk squares have a very small footprint (one tile) and are inexpensive (20 City Coins). To purchase sidewalk squares, click the Decorations tab of the Build menu.

Many people feel that keeping all buildings connected to roads keeps a city better organized and neater looking, such as the one shown in Figure 5-7. Others think that utilizing sidewalks gives them more creative options when configuring their cities, such as the one shown in Figure 5-8.

Figure 5-7: A city built utilizing roads.

If you can't decide which direction you want to go in, why not try both? Maybe on one side of your city, expand it using sidewalks. On the other, place buildings only on roads. Then see which option you like the best.

Figure 5-8: Utilizing sidewalks in your city gives you creative freedom.

Every building must still be connected to the road somehow. If you utilize sidewalks connected to roads to conserve space, each building must be connected to the sidewalk for them to be usable.

Wait to decorate

We know it's tempting to buy the most extravagant-looking items from the Build menu as soon as you can, especially when you have Coins to spare. However, being frugal at first and focusing on more productive uses for your Coins pays. After you build up a few businesses and homes to bring in regular income, you can start utilizing decorations to not only beautify your city but also to increase the payout of those buildings you worked so hard on!

Add neighbors

The more neighbors you have, the more opportunities you have to receive gifts, earn Coins, collect bonuses, and build up your city. In fact, there are many tasks, such as staffing community buildings, that you can't perform if you don't have enough neighbors. For more on adding and interacting with neighbors, see Chapter 6. For more information on community buildings, see Chapter 4.

Watch your Facebook News Feed

Every city slicker could use more Coins, and getting those items for free is a great way to jump-start your profits. You can collect Coin bonus rewards from your CityVille friends by clicking the links they share in their News Feeds (see Figure 5-9). Don't wait too long to click, though. These rewards aren't around for long! While you're at it, be sure to publish bonuses to *your* News Feed to allow your CityVille neighbors to share your bounty.

Figure 5-9: Watch your News Feed for bonuses!

Maximize your time and Energy

Chances are you don't have all day to sit in front of your computer to keep up with all the tasks that need done in your bustling city. That means when you return to your city, you have crops to harvest, rent from homes to collect, profits from businesses to pick up, ships to unload — you get the picture. After all, the city can't restock itself! But how do you make sure you can get everything done in the amount of time you have? Well, you may not be able to. But that doesn't mean you can't get your city on a collection and harvesting schedule to allow you to maximize your time and Energy outputs.

Try planting different crops that ripen at different times of the day. Make sure you have plenty of storage space so you don't run out of Goods all the time. Build homes with different rent collection schedules and businesses that have varying amounts of Goods for sale. Each of these ideas allows you to work on parts of your city at a time. For more information on maximizing your time, Energy, and profits in your city, see Chapter 9.

Upgrade homes as soon as possible

Although you have to start with smaller homes that offer smaller population increases, less rent, and quicker collection times, you don't have to stick with those homes throughout your adventure. As soon as you can afford to, remove these smaller, more Energy point–hogging homes, such as the Cozy Cottage, for homes that offer more population growth, increased profits, and longer collection times, such as the Apartment Complex. Chapter 9 gives more tips on how to find the right mix of residences to fit your city.

Won't You Be My Neighbor?

*A*lthough you can technically play CityVille as a wholly single-player experience, adding some neighbors can definitely enhance your enjoyment of the game. Although a good neighbor can't be purchased for any price, these companions provide priceless benefits. These include tangible benefits such as Coins, Experience Points, and free gifts, and the intangible joys of sharing the CityVille experience with like-minded friends.

This chapter tells you everything you need to know about finding neighbors, using them to their full advantage, and treating them right.

Finding and Adding Neighbors

First things first — before you take advantage of what CityVille neighbors have to offer, you need to get some neighbors! Because signing up to play CityVille is completely free, literally anyone with Internet access is a potential neighbor. Some potential neighbors are likely to be better neighbors than others, however, as we outline here.

Sending neighbor requests to Facebook friends

The friends you've already amassed on your Facebook account are the most obvious source of new CityVille neighbors. In fact, any potential neighbor must first become your Facebook friend before they can become your CityVille neighbor. For more on finding and adding Facebook friends, we recommend *Facebook For Dummies* by Carolyn Abram and Leah Pearlman.

So maybe you have friends who enjoy playing one of Zynga's other games, such as Mafia Wars or FarmVille, but they haven't jumped on the CityVille bandwagon yet. Or you have friends playing CityVille already and you didn't even know it. Zynga makes it easy for you to identify and invite these friends to join you in CityVille by adding tabs to help you sort your friends list! To do this:

1. **Click the Invite Friends tab above the CityVille play area.**

   The Invite Friends page appears, as shown in Figure 6-1.

   You can also access this page by clicking the Add Friend icon in the neighbor bar at the bottom of the play area.

2. **Click one of the sub-tabs to filter your friends list:**

   • The *My Active Zynga friends tab* lists those of your Facebook friends that play other Zynga games like Mafia Wars or Café World.

   • The *All Friends tab* is, well, all your Facebook friends.

   • The *CityVille Friends tab,* as shown in Figure 6-1, contains your Facebook friends who currently play CityVille.

   These guys are the most likely to accept your neighbor invitation.

   • The *FarmVille Friends tab* contains those friends who currently don rubber boots and shovel pig slop in FarmVille. Be a pal and invite them over to warm and cozy CityVille! No pig slop, we promise.

3. **Click the names of up to 50 friends you want to invite to play CityVille.**

   You can type all or part of a friend's name in the text box at the top of the list to find a specific friend.

   Friends who are already your CityVille neighbors don't appear in any list.

4. **Click the blue Send CityVille Invitation button.**

   A confirmation window appears.

5. **(Optional) Click the Add Personal Message link to add a note with your request.**

Figure 6-1: The Invite Friends page.

6. Click the blue Send button.

A post appears on your friend's notification menu asking her to join you in playing CityVille. If she clicks the Accept button, she's asked to install the game and set up her city, as discussed in Chapter 2.

Neighbor requests are just that: requests. Your Facebook friend has to click the Accept button on his Game Requests page, as shown in Figure 6-2, before he's officially your neighbor and appears in the neighbor bar at the bottom of your CityVille game. Until he accepts your neighbor invite, he appears in the Neighbor Request Pending section of your My Neighbors tab, which we discuss in Chapter 3.

Figure 6-2: The Game Requests page.

Some of your Facebook friends may be annoyed if you try to get them to install and play a game they have no interest in, especially if you send multiple requests. Of course, you're free to try and convince your friends that they're missing out by not playing CityVille. Just don't be surprised if your friends don't take to the idea as readily as you might hope. Try not to take it personally if one of your Facebook friends doesn't accept your neighbor request. Most likely, they just don't want to get sucked back in to the potentially addictive world of virtual city life.

It's not you . . . it's them.

Finding more neighbors

So you've already sent a neighbor request to every single one of your CityVille-playing Facebook friends, and yet you *still* want more neighbors? Well, good. This shows you understand the importance of neighbors in helping you get the most out of your CityVille city.

After you exhaust all your existing Facebook friends as potential CityVille neighbors, there's only one option for increasing your neighbor count — finding some new friends! Luckily, there are better ways to find potential neighbors than hanging out in a dark bar or posting a personal ad in the paper ("Single white female seeks open-minded partner interested in opening a franchise in my virtual city . . . ."). Instead, there are many places you can go to online to find like-minded players looking for more neighbors:

- ✔ **Zynga's Official forums host an entire thread devoted to connecting people who are looking for new neighbors.** You can find this thread by visiting `http://forums.zynga.com/forumdisplay.php?f=526`. There, you can post a link to your Facebook profile page so people can send you Facebook friend and CityVille neighbor requests, or you can simply use the existing links to send requests of your own to hundreds of willing potential neighbors. Be sure to read the forum rules before you start posting in these forums. You can also navigate to the CityVille Facebook Page at `www.cityville.com` where you can find a list of the available CityVille forums on the left side of the Page.

- ✔ **Check out Facebook itself**. Simply type **CityVille neighbor** into the search box on your Facebook home page and you'll find a list of dozens of Facebook groups where like-minded people gather to look for new neighbors, as shown in Figure 6-3. You can post a note in these groups asking others to add you as a Facebook friend and CityVille neighbor, or click a person's name and send a friend request directly.

Whenever you send a friend request to a stranger, add a note in the request saying that you're interested in becoming CityVille neighbors. That person will be more likely to accept if they know the reason why a stranger is contacting them!

Figure 6-3: A listing of some CityVille neighbor-finding groups on Facebook.

Before you start adding strangers as friends on your Facebook account, consider what this means to the security of your Facebook account and your personal information. By default, these new friends can view any information you post on Facebook — even information you want to limit only to real friends — and can send you messages and post on your Wall as well.

Luckily, you can set privacy and security setting for these CityVille "stranger neighbors" separately from the settings for the rest of your Facebook friends. To do so, follow these steps.

1. **Click the Friends bookmark on the left sidebar of your Facebook home page.**

   The Friends page appears.

2. **Click the Edit Friends button located at the top-right corner of the Friends page.**

   The Edit Friends page appears, showing a list of all your current friends.

3. **Click the Create a List button located at the top right.**

   The Create New List dialog box appears.

4. **Type a name for your new list in the text box.**

   Make the name something applicable and memorable, such as *CityVille-only friends* or *Stranger Neighbors*.

5. **Click the names of any friends you want to add to this list.**

   If you already have some stranger neighbors as Facebook friends, you can add them to your new list by clicking their pictures. You can also add them later, if you prefer.

6. Click the Create List button.

A page for your new list appears. You can access this page at any time by returning to the Edit Friends page in Step 2 and clicking the name of the list in the left sidebar.

7. Type all or part of the name of the stranger neighbor you want to add to the list in the text box.

A drop-down list of all the Facebook friends who match that name appears as you type.

8. Click the name of the stranger neighbor you want to add to the list.

The stranger neighbor is added to the list and appears below the text entry field.

Alternatively, you can click the Add Multiple button, click the faces of as many friends as you want, and then click the Save List button to speed up the process.

9. Repeat Steps 7 and 8 as often as necessary until all your stranger neighbors have been added to the list.

If you add more strangers as Facebook friends later, you have to actively add them to this list by starting from Step 7. You can also do this directly when you accept a friend request by clicking the Add to List button after accepting the request, selecting the stranger neighbor list, and clicking the blue Save button.

10. Choose Account⇨Privacy Settings in the upper-right corner.

The Choose Your Privacy Settings page appears.

11. Click the Customize Settings link below your current settings.

The Customize Settings page appears, as shown in Figure 6-4.

Figure 6-4: The Customize Settings page.

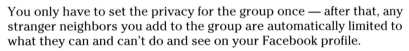

12. **In the drop-down list for each setting you want to restrict, choose Custom.**

    A Custom Privacy dialog box appears asking which people you want this information to be visible or hidden from.

13. **In the Hide This From area, type all or part of the name of the stranger neighbor list and then click the name of that list when it appears.**

    The list appears in the Hide This From area.

14. **Click the Save Setting button.**

    Repeat Steps 12 and 13 until you've set the privacy to your liking.

    You only have to set the privacy for the group once — after that, any stranger neighbors you add to the group are automatically limited to what they can and can't do and see on your Facebook profile.

Removing neighbors

You may have a maximum of 300 CityVille neighbors at a time, and you should do everything you can to hit that limit. Although managing 300 neighbors might seem tough, keep in mind that having a lot of neighbors increases your ability to receive free gifts, such as the ever-important Energy Batteries and building permits, and to take part in in-game activities that require neighbors, as we discuss later in this chapter. Even if you max out your Neighbors list, note that only 50 neighbors display in your neighbor bar at the bottom of the play area, and you can visit only up to 50 neighbors' cities per day.

Not all neighbors are created equal, however. Oftentimes a neighbor agrees to your request and then never visits your city, sends a gift, participates in a community building opportunity, or does anything else to help you out. Other times neighbors stop playing CityVille after accepting your request, clogging up your Neighbors list with static or empty cities.

Just because a Facebook friend has installed CityVille doesn't mean she's still actively playing the game. Look for friends listed with a high CityVille level and number of neighbors on the My Neighbors page because they're most likely to be regular players.

These inactive neighbors are still minimally useful — you can still visit their cities and receive Coins and reputation rewards for helping out, even if that help will go unappreciated. Still, as you near your 300-neighbor limit (or if you just want to clean things up), you may want to cull some of the dead weight from your Neighbors list. You can do this from the My Neighbors page by clicking the red Delete button next to any current neighbor, as shown in Figure 6-5.

Figure 6-5: Be careful when you press the Delete button.

You don't get a confirmation for this kind of neighbor removal, so you have to send another neighbor request if you mis-click. Be careful!

Being a Good Neighbor

Working in your neighbors' cities when there's so much to do in your own city might seem silly, but don't be fooled. Visiting and helping your neighbors' cities is a great way to earn some extra City Coins, Reputation Hearts, and free Goods to take back with you to supply your own businesses, not to mention Experience Points (XP) and Energy bonuses!

Visiting your neighbors' cities

To visit a neighbor's city, simply click that neighbor's image in the neighbor bar at the bottom of the play area and then choose Visit from the menu that appears. A message tells you the neighbor's city is loading, and before you know it, you have a bird's-eye view of your neighbor's domain.

To return to your city at any time, click the Return Home button just above the Tools menu, as shown in Figure 6-6.

It can take a few seconds for your neighbor's city to load completely. Some items on the neighbor's city may appear as shadows for a while, only to pop suddenly into existence as the data is downloaded from Zynga's server.

Helping your neighbor's city

Helping in your neighbor's city isn't exactly like working in your own city — you're actually quite limited in the actions you can take to help your neighbor. Each action comes with a reward of 1 Reputation Heart and 25 Coins (with the exception of harvesting crops), so no matter what you do, you always leave with something for your work!

You can complete only 5 of these tasks in aggregate per neighboring city per 12 hours, as symbolized by the lightning bolts on the left of the play area when visiting a neighbor's city. For example, you could harvest two crops, collect rent from two homes, and send tourists to one of their businesses before having to move on to another city. If there are no lightning bolts on the left of the play area, you have to wait a little longer before providing more help. The following are some of the tasks you can complete:

✔ **Harvest crops:** Click any ripe crop in your neighbor's farm area to harvest that crop. Harvesting a neighbor's farm earns you 15 Goods and 1 Reputation Heart per harvested crop.

Figure 6-6: The Return Home button.

✔ **Revive withered crops:** Click any withered crop in your neighbor's farm area to bring it back to life.

You can't harvest a newly revived crop immediately after reviving it. Go figure.

✔ **Water crops:** Click any unripened crop to water it, and you and your neighbor may get a special surprise — watering crops speeds up their ripening time by one hour. If the crop is within an hour of being ripe, watering it automatically ripens it!

✔ **Collect rent from homes:** Click any home with a Coin icon above it, as shown in Figure 6-7, to collect rent from that home.

You get the usual reward of 25 Coins for this action; the actual rent for that home goes to your neighbor, as normal.

Figure 6-7: Click a home with a coin above it to collect rent.

✔ **Send tourists to businesses:** Clicking businesses with the Trolley icon above them sends a busload of tourists to your neighbor's business, boosting sales without using any of your neighbor's Goods.

✔ **Help build buildings:** If you see that your neighbor has partially completed homes or stores, you can click them once to take them one step close to completing it.

You can't assist your neighbors with building community buildings or their franchise headquarters.

✔ **Unload ships:** Click a loaded ship on your neighbor's pier to unload that ship for that neighbor. See Chapter 7 for more on shipping.

✔ **Clean up spoiled Goods:** Sometimes your neighbor has neglected to unload his ships, and the Goods have spoiled and are floating in the water near their boats, as shown in Figure 6-8. By clicking the ships, you can reload the Goods.

Although you don't have to click the Coins, Hearts, and Goods boxes that appear when you perform a helpful task, doing so quickly activates the Bonus bar, as discussed in Chapter 7. If you're fast (and a little lucky with the loading), you can even keep this Bonus bar going up between multiple neighbor visits.

Figure 6-8: Cleaning up spoiled Goods.

Earning daily visitation bonuses

On top of the bonuses you get for performing specific tasks in a neighbor's city, you also get a bonus of 50 City Coins, 1 Energy, and 1 Experience Point just for showing up. When you visit a new neighbor for the first time, you get a massive bonus of 500 City Coins, 10 Energy, and 10 Experience Points. Note that you can only receive this bonus once per neighbor per day, and only for as many neighbors as your Reputation level (see the "Earning Reputation Hearts and levels" section later in the chapter). Still, these bonuses can be an important way to increase your personal stats, especially Energy, which is otherwise very hard to obtain (see Chapter 7).

Accepting help from neighbors

When you return to your city after a neighbor helps you, you see his hovering avatar and a blue outline surrounding the areas where he helped. Click the avatar to bring up a menu letting you accept or reject that help, as shown in Figure 6-9. For example, if you see your neighbor harvested a crop that you were growing to complete a goal, by clicking Cancel, your neighbor's help will be declined and your crops are safe for you to harvest.

If you reject his assistance this time, it's gone for good. You have to wait until he stops by again to enjoy the benefits. Your neighbor doesn't, however, know whether you reject his help.

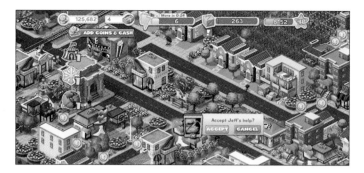

Figure 6-9: Accept or reject your neighbor's help.

The best part about accepting neighborly help is that you don't have to use any Energy from your Energy meter, yet you still reap the full benefits as if you had done the deeds yourself. The only reason to reject this neighborly help is if you need to perform a task yourself to complete a goal.

If you perform the same task as your neighbor did *before* officially accepting his help, the help your neighbor provided is rendered moot. For this reason, be sure to accept neighborly help before performing any other tasks on your city. The only exception comes when accepting help with a harvest — if your Goods storage is already full, supply some of your businesses before accepting the help.

There are many tasks that you can perform to provide neighborly assistance. These include

- **Giving and receiving gifts:** Who doesn't love free stuff? Giving and receiving free gifts is one of the most important roles for a good neighbor.

  See the section "Giving and Accepting Gifts," later in this chapter for more on sending and receiving gifts.

- **Accepting positions in community buildings:** To complete many of the community buildings that increase your population cap, you need help from your neighbors to fill job positions in that building. The number of positions you need filled depends on the building you select, but as a general rule, buildings that raise your population cap more require more positions to be filled. Like all help options in CityVille, accepting positions in community buildings is a two-way street. Accepting help requests from your neighbors is a good idea because they're more likely to return the favor. See Chapter 4 for more information on filling positions in community buildings.

✔ **Gifting wish list items:** When you head to the My Neighbors tab at the top of the playing area, often there are icons next to the person's avatar, such as the ones shown in Figure 6-10. These are the items your neighbor has on his or her wish list. The black number on the top right corner of the icon indicates the number of that item you have in your inventory. See Chapter 3 for more information on wish lists.

Click the green Gift button underneath each icon to send that gift to your neighbor, but be cautious. Unlike sending items from the Free Gifts menu, wish list gift items are actually removed from your inventory! Only give wish list gift items if you really have an excess number of that item.

Figure 6-10: Your neighbor's wish list.

✔ **Selling Goods via the train:** More neighbors mean more potential sources of free Goods for your city's stores, which leads to more purchases and more Coins in your pocket, which leads to the ability to build more stores and homes and, well . . . you get the idea. When you receive notification that a neighbor wants to buy Goods from you, don't let the initial number of requested Goods scare you. When you click the Accept button, you can raise or lower the number of Goods you'll sell to her. That way you can give as much or as little as you can afford to part with. The next time you utilize the train to purchase Goods, your neighbors will return the favor. Chapter 7 goes into more detail on utilizing the train for commerce.

✔ **Completing goals**: Certain goals require you to utilize your neighbor's city. For example, one goal requires you to chop down five of your neighbor's trees in a new land expansion. Not only does this allow you to fulfill your goal but you also save them Energy in the process! Keep an eye out for tree-cutting opportunities and, if possible, leave your new land expansions tree-filled for a day or two to give your neighbors a chance to play lumberjack on your expansion.

✔ **Sharing items and bonuses through News Feed links:** Neighbors can share free items and bonuses by posting links to their Facebook News Feed, which we mention many times throughout this book. See the "Posting Items and Bonuses to a Facebook News Feed" section, later in this chapter for more details on how to post and take advantage of News Feed links.

City etiquette

Ideally, the perfect CityVille neighbor would visit each of her friends' cities daily, completing as many neighborly tasks as she could on each one and pocketing a whole lot of Coins, Goods, and Experience Points in the process. In practice, this might not be feasible for players who have limited time to play.

Even if you can't visit daily, it's still important to do your part to create and maintain a good relationship with each one of your neighbors. If you strive to be a thoughtful neighbor, chances are that your neighbors will return the favor.

Here are several ways to help your neighbors:

- **Construct community buildings:** Neighbors can send each other building materials, such as ribbon and gold plating, for community buildings, saving each other from spending lots of City Cash. See the "Giving and Accepting Gifts" section later in this chapter for more on sending gifts, or see Chapter 4 for more on constructing community buildings.

- **Expand your city:** Although you can purchase the ability to expand your city with City Coins at any time, you also need a certain number of building permits to complete those expansions. The more expansions you've done means you need an even higher amount of building permits the next time you want to expand. Continually supplying your neighbors with building permits by sending these as free gifts ensures they always have enough to build their city when the time comes without spending valuable City Cash. See Chapter 4 for additional information on land expansions.

- **Harvest Goods:** If you only have time to do one task on a neighbor's city, this is it. Not only do you get 1 Reputation Heart and 15 Goods for yourself, but you save him from spending valuable Energy harvesting crops. Harvesting is also important because crops eventually wither, so if your neighbor can't harvest those crops in time, he loses the resulting Goods and Experience Points. See Chapters 5 and 9 for more information on farming.

- **Unwither crops:** If your neighbors can't get back to their city to harvest their crops before they wither, you can use your five tasks to unwither some of their crops. This is one of the few neighborly visit tasks that is impossible for a city manager to perform on his own. You don't get the benefit of collecting extra Goods as you would have if you harvested them, but you did them a favor by giving them back the opportunity to harvest their crops.

✔ **Give and you shall receive:** Sending free gifts is a great way to encourage your neighbors to send free gifts in return. Not only does the game provide a link to return the favor right on the CityVille Messages tab (see Chapter 3), but it also makes that neighbor more likely to think positively of you and want to reward you for your help. If you're in doubt about what gift to give, Energy Batteries are always appreciated!

✔ **Send a return gift after you receive a gift (always):** If you have a reputation for returning gifts when you receive them, your neighbors are more likely to send you gifts out of the blue.

✔ **Share the wealth:** Whenever the game asks whether you want to share a free item or bonus on your Facebook Wall, take advantage of the opportunity. This increases your reputation as a generous neighbor while also letting you brag about your in-game accomplishments.

Helping Your Neighbors

Being a good CityVille neighbor is a two-way street. Not only can those neighbors help you by sending free items, unloading cargo ships, and accepting positions in your community buildings, among other tasks, but you're also expected to do the same things to help those neighbors.

Luckily, CityVille provides bonuses in the form of Reputation Hearts, free Goods, or City Coins for helping your neighbors, thus proving that you can indeed do well by doing good. Read on for all the things CityVille neighbors can do for each other, and what benefits they get for doing so.

Earning Reputation Hearts and levels

Reputation points, or *Reputation Hearts,* are the heart and soul of your interaction with your neighbors. Get it? Heart and soul? Whatever you want to call them, they're very important to your CityVille adventure. All you have to do to get these Reputation Hearts is perform tasks in your neighbors' cities. Every task performed gets you one Reputation Heart added to your Reputation meter, which is shown in Figure 6-11.

Figure 6-11: Your Reputation meter.

The following list spells out what you find on your Reputation meter:

- **Bar number:** The number in the bar shows your total Reputation Hearts earned.

- **Heart number:** The number in the heart shows your current Reputation level.

  The maximum Reputation level you can get is 50, to correspond with the maximum 50 neighbors that can be in your neighbor bar.

- **Red area:** The red area of the bar shows how far you are from reaching the next Reputation level.

  You can hover your mouse pointer over the bar to see precisely how many more Reputation Hearts you need.

What are Reputation Hearts and levels good for? We're glad you asked. Here are the three main benefits:

- **Bonus Goods:** For each new Reputation level you reach, you earn a certain number of bonus Goods, as shown in Table 6-1. As of this writing, the highest Reputation level you can attain is Level 50.

  These Goods are added to your total as soon as you reach the new level, and if you don't have enough storage capacity to hold them all, some will be wasted. If you get close to a new Reputation level, go back to your city and clear some Goods storage space to maximize your bonus. See Chapter 7 for more details on storing Goods.

- **Bonus Energy (when gaining levels):** When you earn enough Experience Points to reach a new level in your city, you receive an immediate Energy bonus equal to your current Reputation level. For example, if reach Level 50 in your city, but your Reputation level is only at 15, you get 15 Energy points in your Energy meter. For more information on gaining levels and using Energy in your city, see Chapter 7.

  If you help your neighbors in their cities for only one reason, Energy is it.

- **More bonuses for neighbor visits:** You can earn bonuses of Coins, Energy, and Experience Points just for visiting your neighbors once every 23 hours. However, the number of times you can receive this bonus in a day is limited by your Reputation level. For example, if your Reputation level is 15, you receive a bonus only for the first 15 neighbors you visit that day. You can still visit more friends and earn Coins and Goods by doing tasks in their cities, but you can't earn the visitation bonus again until 23 hours have passed.

Table 6-1	Reputation Levels and Goods Awarded		
Reputation Level	**Total Hearts Accumulated**	**Total Times Neighbors Helped**	**City Goods Awarded**
1	0	0	0
2	10	2	40
3	25	5	60
4	45	9	80
5	70	14	100
6	100	20	120
7	200	40	140
8	300	60	160
9	400	80	180
10	500	100	200
11	600	120	220
12	700	140	240
13	800	160	260
14	900	180	280
15	1,000	200	300
16	1,100	220	320
17	1,200	240	340
18	1,300	260	360
19	1,400	280	380
20	1,500	300	400
21	1,750	350	420
22	2,000	400	440
23	2,500	500	460
24	3,000	600	480
25	3,500	700	500
26	4,000	800	520
27	4,500	900	540
28	5,000	1,000	560

(continued)

Table 6-1 *(continued)*

Reputation Level	Total Hearts Accumulated	Total Times Neighbors Helped	City Goods Awarded
29	6,000	1,200	580
30	7,000	1,400	600
31	8,000	1,600	620
32	9,000	1,800	640
33	10,000	2,000	660
34	11,000	2,200	680
35	12,000	2,400	700
36	13,000	2,600	720
37	14,000	2,800	740
38	15,000	3,000	760
39	16,000	3,200	780
40	17,000	3,400	800
41	18,000	3,600	820
42	19,000	3,800	840
43	20,000	4,000	860
44	21,000	4,200	880
45	22,000	4,400	900
46	23,000	4,600	920
47	24,000	4,800	940
48	25,000	5,000	960
49	30,000	6,000	980
50	35,000	7,000	1,000

Giving and Accepting Gifts

Sending free gifts is one of the most rewarding things CityVille neighbors can do for one another. Players can save a significant amount of City Cash by receiving Energy Batteries, decorations, and construction materials as free gifts rather than purchasing them from the Build menu.

Even if your neighbor doesn't have an immediate need for a specific gift, he can still sell that gift for some extra City Coins or store it in his inventory until it's needed. For this reason, you should send something to each of your neighbors as often as possible.

Giving gifts

To send free gifts to your neighbors, follow these steps:

1. **Click the Free Gifts tab located above the CityVille game area.**

   The Free Gifts page appears, as shown in Figure 6-12.

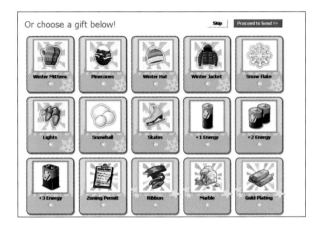

Figure 6-12: The Free Gifts page.

2. **Select the radio button underneath the gift you want to give.**

   You can choose only one gift to give at a time. If you want to give a separate gift to another neighbor, you can repeat this process.

3. **Click either of the blue Proceed to Send buttons at the bottom or top of the free gifts list.**

   The Friend Selection page appears.

4. **Select the check boxes next to the friends you want to send the gift to.**

   You can click the CityVille Friends tab to limit the list only to people who have installed CityVille on their Facebook account. You can send gifts to other Facebook friends, but they have to install the game before they can accept them.

   You can also type all or part of a friend's name into the text box above the friends list to find a particular friend quickly.

To remove a friend, click the X next to their name in the lower portion of the friend selection area.

5. Click the blue Send Gift Request button.

A pop-up notification asks you to send or cancel your gift.

6. Click the blue Send button.

You return to your city. A post detailing your gift appears on your neighbor's Facebook notification menu, Game Requests page, and in the CityVille Message tab. They then have to accept the gift by using the method we outline in the next section.

You can send up to a maximum of 40 free gifts, in aggregate, to your CityVille neighbors in a 23-hour period. However, you can give as many wish list items as you have in your inventory to your neighbors. See Chapter 3 for more information on wish lists.

If you're looking for a specific giftable item for yourself, try sending that same item to a few of your neighbors. Chances are you'll receive multiple thank you gifts of the same type in return.

Accepting and using gifts

Unlike real life, where you're usually just handed a wrapped box, as the recipient of a CityVille gift, you have to actively accept that gift before you can use it. To accept any and all gifts you've been sent, follow these steps:

1. Click the CityVille Messages tab in the upper-right corner of the CityVille play area.

This white tab with a red conversation bubble displays the number of pending requests you have waiting to be accepted. If you have gifts, the number of gifts you have appears in a blue circle next to the tab. If a zero appears, you currently have no pending gifts to accept, so tell your neighbors to get off their butts and send you something, darn it!

2. Click the Accept This Gift button next to each gift received.

The gifts received section is below the neighbor request pending (see Figure 6-13). You also can ignore the gift, but why would you? It's a free gift! Remember, you can always sell an unwanted gift for City Coins, store it in your inventory for later, or use it to fulfill your neighbors' wish lists.

3. (Optional) Click the Want to Send One Back? button.

After you accept the gift, you can send one back to your neighbor. Although this step isn't strictly necessary, sending gifts back to neighbors that send you gifts is a good way to ensure you get more gifts in the future. Remember, helping neighbors is a two-way street!

Figure 6-13: You have gifts!

4. **Repeat Step 2 and, optionally, Step 3 for each gift you received.**

5. **After you're finished accepting gifts, click the Play tab.**

   The familiar CityVille play area appears.

6. **Choose My Stuff⇨Inventory.**

   The My Stuff menu is symbolized by the present and cardboard box on your bottom menu bar.

   Your menu appears with everything you have at your disposal. Consider this your CityVille safety deposit box!

7. **Click the gift to use it (for Energy Batteries) or place it (for decorations and buildings).**

   If you click a decoration or building in your inventory, you immediately return to your city to place it. If you were lucky enough to receive an Energy Battery, clicking it immediately adds that amount of Energy to your Energy meter.

   You don't have to click intangible items, such as building permits or gold plating for community buildings; they remain in your inventory to be used automatically when they're needed.

You can also accept gifts your neighbors send by clicking the Game Requests bookmark on the left side of your Facebook home page, as shown in Figure 6-14, to access the Game Requests page, as shown in Figure 6-15. You can't, however, send back a gift when you utilize this option.

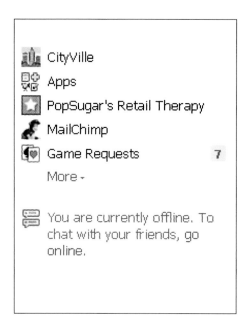

Figure 6-14: The Game Requests bookmark.

Figure 6-15: The Game Requests page where you can accept gifts.

Gifts expire two weeks after they're sent. If you try to accept a gift after this time, you receive nothing but a message urging you to accept your gifts sooner next time. You'd be wise to take that advice.

Operating Franchises in Neighboring Cities

Have you ever dreamed about opening a franchise of your favorite restaurant or store? Now's your chance, albeit only in CityVille. Franchises are yet another way to help neighbors and earn more City Coins with very little work on your part.

The neat thing about franchises is that they can play as big or as little part of your city as you choose. Some people choose to open a few franchises just to complete certain in-game goals (see Chapter 8), and some choose to offer multiple franchise spots in their own city to any and all neighbors who want to get in on the action.

Depending on the level you're at in the game, you're initially limited on the number of franchises you can open. You start with the ability to open one franchise, and that number increases by one after you hit Levels 20, 30, 40, 50, and 60. You can place one franchise lot for every three neighbors you have up to 20 franchise lots.

Getting started in franchising

Franchises are a win-win situation in CityVille. The person hosting the franchise gets to enjoy up to one free Goods supply "fill up" per day from the franchise owner, all the while taking in the money like he would with any other store in his city. An added perk is that neither the franchise owner nor the franchise host has to expend any Energy to build the building — it's a freebie!

Starting a franchise in a neighbor's city

Begin your entrepreneurial expansion with a few simple steps:

1. **Find and click an empty plot in a neighbor's city.**

   You can find these either by scouring your Facebook game requests for new franchise availability notices, or by searching your neighbors' cities for empty plots like the one shown in Figure 6-16. If your neighbor has a very large, packed city, you may have to bring out your magnifying glass to find these plots!

   After clicking an empty franchise plot, the Build menu appears at the bottom of the play area.

   If you're lucky, you neighbor will have a Visitor's Center Community Building that shows you whether she has any franchise plots available before you spend a lot of time searching her city. Your neighbor may not have a Visitor's Center, however so you may end up scouring the city anyway! The Visitor's Center as well as other community buildings are discussed in Chapter 4.

2. **Choose the store you want to place.**

   Only the stores that you have unlocked based on your level appear, as shown in Figure 6-17. (For more on earning levels and unlocking buildings, see Chapter 7.) If you've purchased a specialty store using City Cash, that store appears as well, regardless of your game level. Good news! Franchise stores are available at 20 percent off their usual price! Who doesn't love a bargain?

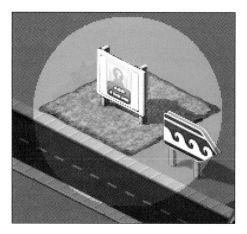

Figure 6-16: An empty plot in a neighbor's city that's ready for your franchise.

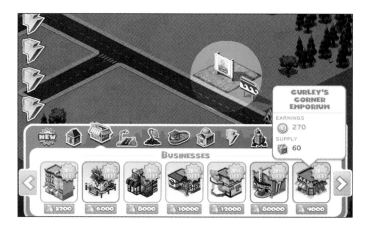

Figure 6-17: A selection of franchises in your Build menu.

3. **Click to place your new franchise under the big yellow arrow.**

Be sure to position your store so there's a green square under it, as shown in Figure 6-18. This ensures it's connected to the street so the residents can get to it. The Toy Store in Figure 6-18 isn't yet in the correct position, as shown by the image of the street covered by a red circle with a line through it.

Figure 6-18: Be sure to position your franchise store correctly.

4. **(Optional) In the box that pops up, click the Share button to post a message to your neighbor's Wall asking her to approve your franchise.**

   You may not want to post a message or you may not be able to, depending on your neighbor's privacy settings. Don't worry, though, your neighbor still sees your request to place a franchise via your avatar hovering over the empty plot the next time she visits her city.

Your new franchise appears as an inactive, faded-out building until your neighbor actively approves it. If this neighbor doesn't log on to CityVille very frequently, it may be a good idea to post a message to her Wall if you can. You may also rethink your choice of a neighbor! After your franchise is approved, you're notified via a post on your Wall.

Placing your franchise headquarters

For each distinct type of franchise you open, you're rewarded with a headquarters (HQ) building for that franchise, as shown in Figure 6-19. As you can see, each headquarters is differentiated by an image on top of the building depicting the type of franchise it represents. The HQ appears in your inventory. To place it, click Inventory under the My Stuff menu, click the building, and then build it like any normal building (see Chapter 5). Each franchise building takes 10 Energy points to build completely, so make sure you save up some Energy to finish it!

The larger the variety of stores you open, the more franchise HQs you can place in your city. If you open multiple franchises of a single store type, the franchise HQ for that store type gains an extra floor. Towering franchise HQs can be a sign of prestige in CityVille and are a great way to make your city stand apart from those of your neighbors, but otherwise the size of an HQ has no effect.

Although placing your franchise HQ somewhere in your city is a nice feather in your cap, it takes up a lot of land and you may not have room for it right away. Don't worry, this doesn't affect how your stores function. Even if you choose not to place your franchise HQ, your stores still show up in your franchise dashboard and you can still supply them and collect from them.

That's it! Congratulations on being a new franchise owner! Now be sure to keep your franchise supplied every day, as we detail in the "Running your franchises" section, later in this chapter. Besides being a great way to earn extra City Coins, a franchise is a nice way to thank your neighbor for allowing you to expand your business empire to his city.

Figure 6-19: Welcome to your new franchise headquarters!

Setting up and approving, or rejecting, a franchise in your city

So you say you're ready to open the gates to your beloved city and allow a neighbor to build a franchise? First of all, good choice! It means less work and more City Coins for you. Win-win, remember? Secondly, how neighborly of you! After you decide to place a lot, you have to decide whether to accept or reject the neighbors interested in putting a store there. Remember, you must choose based on what's best for your city.

But first things first — you must place an Empty Lot in your city. Your first Empty Lot is ready and waiting for you when you start your city and doesn't require any neighbors. But each succeeding Empty Lot you place requires an additional three neighbors before it can be placed. So for example, if you have 12 neighbors, you can put a total of 5 Empty Lots in your city. To get started placing Empty Lots, follow these steps:

1. **Click the Build button at the bottom of the play menu.**

   The Build menu appears at the bottom of the play area.

2. **Select the Business tab, which is the second from the left, and then click the empty lot item, which is the first from the left.**

   The Build menu disappears, and a translucent Empty Lot icon appears under your mouse pointer. The best part? The Empty Lot is free!

3. **Place the empty lot in a location connected to either a road or a sidewalk.**

   Although you can technically place your lot in any spot with enough space, any business on the lot will be useless if it's not connected to a place your residents can reach.

4. **(Optional) Click the Share button on the dialog box that appears to post a message to your Wall asking a friend to open a business in your city.**

   This quickly gets out the word that you're ready for a franchise to move in. If you don't want to post anything to your Wall, that's okay. Neighbors see the Empty Lot when they visit your city.

After you have a neighbor interested in opening a store in your city, here's how you can approve or reject it:

1. **Click the neighbor avatar above the Empty Lot.**

   You're presented with three buttons: Accept, Later, or Decline, as shown in Figure 6-20. If you click Later, you put off making the decision for the time being.

2. **Click the green Accept button or the red Decline button, depending on your decision.**

   If you accept the franchise, a message appears giving you the option to inform your neighbor you approved it and ask whether you want to share a bonus with him. If you decline the franchise, you're asked whether you want to send a thank you gift to your neighbor instead.

3. **Click the Share Coins button if you want to send bonus Coins to your neighbor, or click the X on the top right of the box if you do not.**

   If you decide to share Coins, you can post a message to your neighbor's Wall informing him of your decision to accept or decline his franchise offer.

Figure 6-20: Deciding to accept or reject a franchise request.

Removing franchises

As of the writing of this book, you can't remove a franchise that you have in a neighbor's city, outside of asking her to do it for you. We recommend a polite, straightforward approach to the situation. However, if you find that you spend a lot of time managing franchises that aren't bringing in a lot of money, you may want to just stop supplying them. Eventually your neighbor may decide you're not a good fit for her city and remove your franchise herself.

If you want to remove a franchise that's no longer a fit for *your* city, here's how you go about doing it:

1. **Click the Tools menu in the bottom menu and choose the Remove tool.**

   A confirmation box appears asking whether you really want to sell the building for 0 Coins.

2. **Click the green Yes button.**

   A pop-up box appears, reading `I'm sure your neighbor will understand that their business is no longer a good fit for your city. Would you like to send a thank you gift?`

3. **Click the Share Coins button if you want to send a thank you gift, or click the X on the top right of the box if you do not.**

   If you don't choose to send a thank you gift, your neighbor doesn't receive a notification that her store has been removed; however, it no longer shows up in her Franchise menu.

Running your franchises

After you get up and running with your franchises, it takes only a couple of minutes a day to manage them through the Franchise menu. To bring up this menu, choose My Stuff⇨Franchises.

TIP

You can also access your Franchise menu by clicking any one of your franchise HQ buildings (which we discussed in the "Placing your franchise headquarters" section earlier in this chapter) or by clicking the franchise icon that sometimes appears in the tasks section on the left side of the game play area.

At the top of the Franchise menu are tabs representing all the different types of franchises you own, as shown in Figure 6-21. Each tab includes Collect button to get your a daily bonus as well as a list of the franchises you have in neighboring cities.

Earning City Coins

Clicking the Daily Bonus button under a franchise tab earns you City Coins for each franchise of that type you maintain in neighboring cities, and the amount depends on the level you're at and the particular business. For example, a Flower Shop franchise earns you 25 Coins for each store you own in neighboring cities, but each Bridal Shop franchise you own nets you a 100 City Coin daily bonus! That's right — you get a City Coin bonus just for going to the Franchise menu! You can collect this bonus only once a day for each franchise type. After you collect, the button is replaced with a 23-hour countdown clock, showing how long until your next daily bonus opportunity.

Figure 6-21: All your franchises in one convenient location.

The number of City Coins you earn for each franchise depends on two things: the total payout of that particular store and the number of decorations your neighbor has around the store to increase that payout. For example, if your store has a payout of 700 Coins and your neighbor has decorations around that store that boosts the store's profits by 20 percent, your total payout for that franchise is 840 Coins! Not too shabby, huh?

Supplying franchises

Below the Daily Bonus button is a list of all the franchises of a particular type that you maintain in neighboring cities. Think of this as your franchise dashboard. Click the Supply button next to any specific franchise to supply that franchise with Goods. The number of Goods required for each franchise type differs and is listed in orange in the center column. The number of Goods is immediately deducted from your total. The person who builds the franchise reaps daily bonuses and Coin rewards for supplying each franchise with 50 percent of the Goods needed for a store refill. For example, if you place a Burger Joint in a neighbor's city, every time you supply this franchise, your Goods supply is reduced by 38 while the owner of the city supplies the remaining 37 to make up the difference for the 75 total Goods that are needed.

If your neighbor hasn't yet accepted your last Goods delivery yet (which we discuss in the "Accepting delivery of Goods" section, later in this chapter), the Supply button is replaced with an orange Remind button next to that franchise. Click the Remind button to post a message on his Wall reminding him to accept your shipment of Goods so you both can continue to make money! The Remind button can be clicked only once a day.

Earning franchise stars

The more often you return to supply your store, the more often your neighbor returns to his city and accepts your delivery, the more yellow stars that franchise earns. So if you and your neighbor are active every day for five days, you can earn all five stars! These stars display under your neighbor's name and avatar in the Franchise menu. The number of stars a franchise has acts as a multiplier for the daily proceeds you earn for supplying that franchise. For example, if a franchise has 3 stars and provides a base of 200 Coins for each supply run, you receive 600 City Coins from that franchise every time you supply it!

New franchises start with zero stars. You earn your first star the first time you return to supply them after your franchise offer was accepted by your neighbor.

Accepting delivery of Goods

As soon as your neighbor clicks that Supply button in her Franchise menu, a green tag with a cardboard box and lightning bolt appears above that franchise in your city, as shown in Figure 6-22.

To accept her shipment of Goods, simply click the building. Coins, Goods, and an Energy point are released from the business and can be collected as normal (see Chapter 5 for more on collecting from businesses). After accepting this Goods shipment, you can still collect Coins from the franchise as normal, effectively doubling the productivity for that business.

Figure 6-22: A franchise store was supplied.

Here are a few things to keep in mind when diving into the world of franchises:

- **Not all neighbors are open to franchises.** Some want to keep all their precious land to themselves, which is okay. You may choose to do the same.

- **Not all neighbors will accept your franchise.** Some of your neighbors may have a specific neighbor in mind when they set up an empty franchise plot. Others may prefer to have a business that provides higher returns. Just give yourself a little time to level up more and try again later.

- **Your franchise host can remove your store at any time without notice to you.** Although it's polite for a franchise host to notify the franchise owner that he's going to reclaim his land, not all neighbors do that. You may wake up one day and find you no longer have one of your beloved Shoe Store franchises. If you're lucky, the host will post a message on your Wall notifying you of the intent to reclaim the land so you can at least claim your consolation prize of 50 City Coins. Either way, don't take offense to it. It's his prerogative to use his land how he wants, and one day you may choose to do the same.

- **Some neighbors never come back to supply their franchises**. This means you're stuck supplying those businesses, which ruins most of the point of accepting a franchise. You can choose to keep that store and treat it as your own, accepting that you'll never get that freebie restock from them ever again, or you can bulldoze their franchise to reclaim that land for yourself or a neighbor who will be more engaged.

Posting Items and Bonuses to a Facebook News Feed

While playing CityVille, you have many opportunities to post a message on your Facebook Wall. These news posts can be everything from letting your neighbors know you visited their city to accepting free items to requests for helping staff community buildings.

These opportunities are usually indicated with a Share button or something similar in a pop-up notification window as you play. Clicking this button brings up the Wall publishing box, as shown in Figure 6-23.

Figure 6-23: A Facebook News Feed publishing box.

You can type a message in the text box to add a more personal touch to the basic news post written by CityVille. You can also click the lock next to the Publish button to restrict the news post's visibility to a certain, limited group of your Facebook friends. This can be especially handy for sharing CityVille links only with people you know are interested in playing CityVille.

After you customize the post to your liking, click the Publish button to share the link on your News Feed. You can also click the Skip button to pass up the opportunity to share with your neighbors.

Your neighbors can click the link that appears in their News Feed to accept the item or bonus or to provide help with your request. Note that some items shared via News Feeds are available only for a limited time or are available only to the first few neighbors that click the link. Be sure to click News Feed links shared by your neighbors as soon as possible to take full advantage of these opportunities.

Competing With Your Neighbors: Keeping Up with the Joneses

C'mon, you can admit it! You have a bit of a competitive streak. Or maybe more than a bit. Maybe you have a huge competitive streak. That's okay. We understand. That's what games are all about, right? There's nothing wrong with heading over to your neighbor's city just to look around and see what he's been up to. Maybe his city hasn't changed much since you last visited. Or maybe he's grown his city by leaps and bounds, seemingly overnight. Wait a second, how did the city get so big so fast?!

First of all, relax! Just because he seems to be so far ahead of you now doesn't mean that you can't catch up and close that gap. So what's a city slicker to do? The recipe is simple: Monkey see, monkey do. Pay attention to changes your successful neighbors make and consider making those changes yourself. Play around with techniques to see which ones work the best for you and your schedule. Here are some to consider:

- ✔ **Visit neighbors' cities frequently:** Or as much as your schedule allows. We realize that sometimes it's not possible to log on a few times a day, or even once a day. That means when you do get a chance to head on over, be sure to give their cities a thorough inspection and take note of any new buildings and expansions. Have they increased the amount of farmland they have and started planting a lot of a certain crop? This may mean they found a recipe to success for keeping stocked on Goods. Take that into consider the next time you plant crops.

- ✔ **Keep an eye on their game level, Reputation meter, and City Coins:** Clicking the My Neighbors tab at the top of the game play area gives you a glance into your neighbor's stats, specifically her game level, Reputation level, and how many City Coins she's saved. Chances are you find that your most successful neighbors have high Reputation levels, meaning they not only have many neighbors, but they also visit and help around their neighbor's cities a lot. Follow their lead! If a neighbor has a high game level, he's collected a lot of Experience Points by work-ing hard around his city, so get busy in yours! If he's amassed a large number of City Coins, maybe he's saving for something special in the Build menu that appears only at the higher levels he's at. (We discuss earning Experience Points and game levels more in Chapter 7.) At the very least, you can spy on him and use his success as incentive to work harder. A little friendly competition never hurt anyone, right?

- ✔ **Pay attention to when they work in their cities:** Many players, espe-cially those who have utilized the CityVille forums, have neighbors who live in different countries, and therefore live in different time zones. Pay attention to when you can perform specific tasks in their cities. For example, if you visit them a number of times and notice that their crops seem to ripen at the same time, chances are they're playing the game at the same time every day. Be sure to return to their city during that time to maximize your ability to collect Goods!

- ✔ **Take note of their city's layout:** Do they have a lot of roads, or are most of their buildings connected by sidewalks? Are all their houses clustered together on one side of their city, with community buildings in another section of their city and stores in still another? Setting up their cities like that may mean they're just über-organized, but chances are there's a method to their madness, especially if they're at a high level. For exam-ple, having all your dwellings set up in one area saves precious minutes when collecting rent. Chances are you're going to have as many differ-ent city configurations as you will successful neighbors, so use trial and error to find the way that helps you advance in the game the quickest.

- **For goodness sake, ask!:** Your neighbors have all accepted your neighbor request and engaged in a mutually beneficial relationship with you. That means there's a certain level of trust between the two of you, so why not post a message on their Facebook Wall asking about the secrets to their success. People love when others recognize their accomplishments, so chances are they'll be happy to answer your questions.

  This technique doesn't work if this neighbor has her Facebook privacy settings set so that people from CityVille can't post on her Wall. To check whether you can, try to share awards with them. If you aren't allowed, you receive a message saying that this person doesn't allow you to post messages to her Wall. If that's the case, try another one of your successful neighbors.

- **Visit the CityVille forums:** Keep tabs on the CityVille forums and other Web resources we mention in Chapter 10 to find users posting tips and tricks to advance in the game. Soon you'll be so successful that *you* will be posting to these forums!

Part II
Seeking Your CityVille Fortune

The 5th Wave   By Rich Tennant

"Donny finds it hard playing CityVille without the kickbacks, bribes, and money laundering."

*T*he second part of the book focuses on how to build and maintain a thriving City.

Learn about the various CityVille currencies as well as tips on how to spend your cash wisely in Chapter 7. It also delves into the importance of managing your energy levels in order to advance in the game.

Chapter 8 is all about goals: how they work, how completing them will help you move through the game and how to prioritize them in order to play the game efficiently.

Chapter 9 gives you information on how to build the most efficient City you can through maximizing your land usage, finding the right mix of homes and businesses as well as how to utilize decorations to beautify your space.

Managing Your Resources

In This Chapter

▷ Keeping track of Coins, Cash, Goods, and Energy

▷ Leveling up and unlocking new items

▷ Collecting and storing inventory items

*J*ust like in a real city, the economy is the engine driving the heart of your virtual CityVille city. *Resources,* in turn, are the items that drive that economy, and knowing how to collect them, when to spend them, and when to save them are important to success in the game.

Like a real economy, currency is a major part of the CityVille system of Goods and services. CityVille currency comes in the form of City Cash and City Coins, both of which can be earned either through game play or by making a purchase with real money. This chapter tells you the differences between the currency types, and when to use each.

Goods are another important part of the CityVille resource mix. Generally these Goods are acquired by harvesting crops and used to supply stores that serve your populace. This chapter outlines the best ways to store those Goods and manage your actions so you keep a full complement of Goods ready at all times.

One limited resource that is often overlooked in CityVille is Energy. Your Energy meter limits how many in-game actions you can take over time, and managing it effectively is key to getting the most out of your city as quickly as possible. This chapter discusses how to use your Energy efficiently and get the most out of your clicks.

Finally, this chapter details the game's Experience Points and leveling systems, as well as collectables and other items that go into your inventory. This all may seem like a lot to take in, but don't worry, you'll be an expert at resource management before long.

Earning City Coins and Cash

City Coins and Cash are by far the most important resources in the game. You use them to buy everything from crops to skyscrapers, and for a wide variety of actions. Being able to bring in currency quickly and efficiently, and to turn it into new buildings and decorations, are the keys to running a successful city.

Breaking down the differences between Coins and Cash

In the real world, Coins are just smaller, more portable denominations of paper cash. In CityVille, this couldn't be further from the truth. In fact, City Coins and City Cash are completely different currency systems, with different availability and uses.

City Coins

City Coins are by far the more common type of currency. You start the game with 7,000 of them in your account and earn more for taking any of the following actions:

- **Collecting rent from housing or businesses**: The precise amount varies by building — see Chapter 4.

- **Clicking Coin bonuses posted by neighbors in your Facebook News Feed:** You earn 50 Coins (see Chapter 6 for more on Facebook post bonuses).

- **Clearing withered crops:** You earn half of the original crop purchase price.

- **Chopping down trees:** You earn 25 Coins.

- **Helping neighboring cities**: You earn 50 Coins per visit (100 for the first visit) and 25 Coins per helping action (see Chapter 6).

- **Clicking Resource icons:** The precise amount varies — see the next section.

Performing most of these actions (with the exception of neighbor visits and clicking Facebook bonuses) results in a Coin icon popping out onto the play area. This icon can look like a Coin, but can also look like a money bag, a gold ingot, a shiny diamond, or up to three of any of these items. Which Coin icon displays depends on the amount of Coins you've earned from your action, as shown in Table 7-1.

Table 7-1	City Coin Resource Icons
Clicking This Icon . . .	*. . . Earns This Many City Coins*
	1 to 99
	100 to 199
	200 to 299
	300 to 399
	400 to 599
	600 to 799
	800 to 999
	1,000 to 1,499
	1,500 to 1,999
	2,000 to 2,499
	2,500 to 2,999
	3,000 or more

You can use these icons as a quick visual guide to how many Coins various buildings produce. However, when you click the icon, a small bit of green text tells you exactly how many Coins the icon is worth, as shown in Figure 7-1.

Figure 7-1: The confirmation message shown after clicking a Coin icon worth 100 Coins.

Coins can be used to purchase the vast majority of items in the game, but you might have to save millions of them for some of the more lucrative buildings, as we detail in Chapter 4.

City Cash

City Cash is much rarer than City Coins and, therefore, more coveted. You start the game with five City Cash, and the only way to earn more in the game itself is by earning new levels (see the section "Earning Experience Points and Levels," later in this chapter). You can also purchase more City Cash outside of the game play by spending real cash or completing promotional offers, as we discuss in an upcoming section.

That's the bad news. The good news regarding City Cash is that it can be used to buy lucrative items that can't be had for City Coins. For instance, some of the best buildings and most efficient decorations in the game can be purchased only with City Cash (see Chapters 9 and 12 for more on some of these). City Cash can also be used to

✔ Buy out positions in buildings that would otherwise need staffing by neighbors (see Chapter 6).

✔ Skip tricky requirements on some quests (see Chapter 8).

Because City Cash is so hard to acquire, spend it wisely. In the section "Spending your City Cash wisely," later in this chapter, we have some recommendations on when to spend and when to save.

Getting bonus City Coins for quickly clicking Resource icons

For the most part, playing CityVille doesn't require quick reflexes or fast clicking. The one exception to this rule is the Bonus bar that appears when you start clicking Resource icons in the game.

A *Resource icon,* as we discuss throughout this chapter and the book, is simply an icon that pops up to represent an in-game resource. These icons can be Coins, good boxes, collectables, Energy bolts, or other items.

Clicking any of these Resource icons adds the applicable resource to your account and starts a Bonus bar, as shown in Figure 7-2. This bar flashes red after about three seconds and disappears completely after about six seconds — that is, unless you click another Resource icon before it does. Clicking another Resource icon resets the six-second countdown timer and fills the meter a little bit.

Figure 7-2: The Bonus bar, as it initially appears in the upper-right corner of the play area.

When the Bonus bar fills completely, it moves on to the next bonus level, as indicated by a new exclamatory word. For instance, filling the meter once changes Bonus! to Excellent! When you run out of Resource icons to click and the Bonus bar disappears, you earn a Coin bonus based on the last Bonus bar level you've completed, as detailed in Table 7-2. The size of this bonus is based on a multiplier of your current in-game level, so as you progress in the game, the bonuses get progressively larger.

If you max out at the Masterfull!!! bonus level while still clicking Resource icons, you automatically collect the maximum available Coin bonus of 82.5 times your current level, and then you immediately restart at the starting Bonus! level. For instance, if you click 45 Resource icons without letting the Bonus bar disappear, you first collect the maximum bonus of 82.5 times your current level and then you collect an Amazing! bonus of 9 times your level after you're done.

Table 7-2	Bonus Bar Coin Bonuses	
Bonus Level	Number of Total Resource Icon Clicks Needed to Complete Bonus Level	Coin Reward for Completing Bonus Level
Bonus!	5	1.5 × level
Excellent!	9	4.5 × level
Amazing!	13	9 × level
Outstanding!	17	15 × level
Holy Smokes!	20	22.5 × level
Extreme!	23	31.5 × level
OMGeezers!	26	42 × level
Unstoppable!	28	54 × level
Insane!!	30	67.5 × level
Masterful!!!	32	82.5 × level

As you can see from Table 7-2, keeping your Bonus bar going as long as possible is key to getting large Coin bonuses, especially as you increase you level. To this end, focus on getting as many Resource icons on the play area before you start clicking to collect them. Community buildings are especially good for this purpose because they tend to drop six or seven icons every time they're clicked for collection.

Don't wait too long before you start clicking, though, because Resource icons disappear after about ten seconds on the play field. Don't worry — you still get the resources even if you don't click them in time. Your Bonus bar timer won't reset in this case, however. Mix up clicking buildings and clicking Resource icons if you have to in order to keep the Bonus bar going continuously as you empty your Energy meter completely. (See Chapter 9 for more on planning an effective clicking strategy.)

Buying CityVille currency with real money

Although you can play CityVille without spending a dime on the game, you can also spend real money to give yourself a leg up over the competition. You have several ways to convert your real, legal tender into CityVille currency, including making an in-game credit card purchase and buying a Game Card from a local retailer.

To spend or not to spend real money?

The idea of exchanging legal tender for CityVille's entirely fake currencies is somewhat controversial. Although many players enjoy CityVille without shelling out one shiny red cent for the privilege, Zynga makes hundreds of millions of dollars every year from players who voluntarily use their hard-earned money to buy items that exist only as pixels on a screen and bits in a server.

Many of these paying players spend just a few dollars a month to buy the occasional limited-edition building or to hurry along an especially slow quest. But some players take their spending seriously:

✔ One preteen in the United Kingdom made headlines when he used his mom's credit card (without her permission, needless to say) to purchase almost $1,400 worth of virtual Goods in Zynga's popular FarmVille game, which has a similar currency system.

✔ Zynga even operates a Platinum Purchase Program that accepts wire transfers of $500 and up from truly obsessive players.

As with all decisions regarding your money (except for taxes), what you spend on CityVille is entirely up to you. Everyone has different priorities and tolerances for spending money. Some people like saving their money for a rainy day; others prefer burning through it like there's a hole in their pocket. Whatever decision you make regarding your CityVille spending, you can still have a great time playing the game.

Some food for thought, though: Although a spendthrift player can always decide to buy more CityVille currency later, a player who invests in a lot of CityVille currency can never convert that currency back to real, legal tender. As the ancient Romans used to say, *caveat maior* — let the mayor beware. Okay, they probably never said that, but they would have if they'd had CityVille back then. Trust us.

Buying City Coins and Cash through CityVille

The CityVille developers at Zynga have made buying CityVille currency so easy that you don't even have to leave the game to do it. Click the Add Coins & Cash tab above the CityVille play area to display the Buy City Cash & Coins page, as shown in Figure 7-3.

Follow these steps to add more in-game currency to your account:

1. **Select the amount of City Cash or City Coins that you want to purchase and click the Continue button.**

   A payment option menu appears.

   Spending more money gets you a better in-game exchange rate. Buying the smallest package of City Cash, for instance, gets you 7.5 City Cash per dollar, whereas buying the largest package gets your over 10 City Cash for each of the $99 you spend. That in-game money doesn't go bad, either, so plan ahead and buy in bulk to save.

Figure 7-3: The Add Coins & Cash page.

2. **Select the appropriate radio button to choose whether to pay with a new credit card, a previously used credit card, or a PayPal account and then click Continue.**

   CityVille accepts any valid Visa, MasterCard, American Express, Discover, or JCB card. You can also use a PayPal account; for more on using this option, visit www.paypal.com or check out *PayPal For Dummies,* by Victoria Rosenborg and Marsha Collier.

   If you've purchased or earned any of Facebook's Credits currency, you can select the Apply Existing Balance check box to put those Credits toward your purchase at a rate of 10 cents per Facebook Credit.

   Facebook automatically stores any new credit card information you enter, so you don't have to type it again the next time you want to buy CityVille currency. If you want to delete this information from Facebook for security reasons, choose Account⇔Account Settings in the upper right of your Facebook home page and click the Payments tab.

3. **Enter your credit card information and click the Complete Purchase button, or log in to your PayPal account and click the Agree and Pay button.**

   Note: You skip this step if you use an existing credit card already stored by Facebook.

Why use Game Cards?

You might want to trek to a local store and purchase a Game Card rather than pay for your CityVille currency online. Some reasons to make the trek include the following:

✔ Many people still aren't comfortable sharing their financial information online. Although Facebook and CityVille use encryption technology to secure your online payments, no online payment method is foolproof, and there's always a chance that hackers could somehow obtain your payment and billing information through an online transaction. Buying a Game Card in a brick-and-mortar store is anonymous and lets you keep your personal information personal.

✔ Game Cards are a convenient option for people who don't have access to a credit card or other online payment account.

This applies especially to children, who usually don't have credit cards. Although Mom is likely to be wary of handing her credit card over to the kids, a prepaid Game Card removes the risk of an unauthorized shopping spree.

✔ Gifts! Currently, CityVille lets you use online payments only to add in-game currency to your personal account. If you want to give some City Cash or City Coins to a friend, your only options are to buy a physical Game Card to give them or to purchase a Zynga Game Card online (see the "Sending Zynga Game Cards as online gifts" section, later in this chapter). Just like retail gift cards, Game Cards make great presents for CityVille-lovers.

You know what other present they might enjoy? This book! Why not buy another copy (or 12!)?

City Cash and City Coins are not refundable; you can't convert in-game currency back into cold, hard cash. After you click the Complete Purchase or Agree and Pay button, your money can be used only in CityVille, so make sure you don't actually need that cash to pay your mortgage, gas bill, or something else before continuing.

After your payment processes, your City Cash or City Coins are added to your current total. The purchased currency usually appears in your CityVille account pretty promptly, but it can take a few hours or even a few days for your currency purchase to appear. If your purchased currency doesn't appear after a few days, see Chapter 10 for details on contacting Zynga support for help.

An alternative to paying online: CityVille Game Cards

If you're unwilling or can't use any of the online payment methods, you can purchase CityVille Game Cards at many brick-and-mortar retailers. You can then redeem these cards online for CityVille currency. Although using Game Cards to get CityVille currency is decidedly less convenient than using the online payment methods, you might want to consider it, as discussed in the nearby "Why use Game Cards?" sidebar.

Where to buy CityVille Game Cards

As of this writing, CityVille Game Cards are stocked at the following retailers:

- 7-Eleven
- Best Buy
- CVS
- Duane Reade
- GameStop
- Rite Aid
- Target
- Walmart
- Walgreens

Redeeming CityVille Game Cards

When you purchase your CityVille Game Card, you need to have it activated at checkout. You then need to redeem it for CityVille currency online. To do so, click the GameCards tab above the CityVille play area to bring up the Redeem Card page, as shown in Figure 7-4. Then follow these steps to redeem your card:

1. **Enter the PIN code from the card in the Enter PIN Code box.**

   You find this code on the back of your Game Card.

2. **Click the Next Step button.**

   A confirmation screen appears. Your City Cash is automatically added to your existing City Cash bank. Simple!

Figure 7-4: The Redeem Card page.

Sending Zynga Game Cards as online gifts

In addition to buying a CityVille Game Card at a brick-and-mortar retailer, you can also purchase a Zynga Game Card online as a gift. These virtual cards technically work for any Zynga game, but can be personalized to feature CityVille.

To give a Zynga Game Card as an online gift:

1. **Enter** www.zynga.com/gamecards **in the address box of your Web browser and press Enter.**

2. **On the page that appears, click the Give a Card link on the left sidebar.**

   The Give an eCard menu opens, as shown in Figure 7-5.

Figure 7-5: The Give an eCard menu.

3. **Choose your preferred Game Card amount from the drop-down list.**

   Zynga Game Cards are currently available in denominations of $10, $15, $25, and $50. You can also use the drop-down list to choose Canadian dollars (CAD) and British pounds (GBP).

4. **Click the Game Card design you want to give.**

   Click the left and right arrows to scroll through the available designs. You can also use the drop-down list to limit the choices to designs for a certain occasion, such as a birthday or a thank you gift.

5. **Fill out the Game Card information and click the Continue button.**

   You can choose for the Game Card to be delivered at a future date, which is convenient if you're planning ahead for a special event. Also note that the personal message can't be more than 400 characters, including spaces.

6. **Fill in your credit card information or click the PayPal button to pay with your PayPal account; then click the Purchase button.**

   If you're not comfortable using these payment options, consider getting a CityVille Game Card from a local retailer (see the previous section, "An alternative to paying online: CityVille Game Cards").

Your Game Card gift appears in the recipient's e-mail box on the date you chose in Step 5. Redeeming an e-mailed Zynga Game Card works the same as redeeming a physical CityVille Game Card, except that you find the PIN number in the e-mail message rather than on the back of the card. See the preceding section "Redeeming CityVille Game Cards" for more details on redeeming Game Cards.

Spending your City Cash wisely

With City Cash being such a valuable, hard-to-replace commodity, it's not a good idea to spend it as freely as City Coins, which can be replaced quite easily. Think long and hard before making any City Cash purchase.

Here are some tips to consider before throwing away your hard-earned Cash:

- **Consider City Coin alternatives:** Although many of the game's best buildings and decorations can be had only for a dear sum of City Cash, some of these items are actually no better than their plainer, City Coin alternatives. For instance, the 45 City Cash Courtyard House has the exact same population and rent statistics as the Skyscraper Condos, which cost 500,000 City Coins. The Courtyard House may seem a lot cheaper, on a purely numeric basis, but when you consider how much easier it is to get a lot of City Coins, the Skyscraper Condo is probably the better deal.

- **Be patient:** CityVille is full of opportunities to spend City Cash to speed up the game. These include spending Cash to

  - Fill necessary positions in community buildings (see Chapter 6).

  - Attain the requisite building permits needed to expand the town.

  In all these cases, you can always save your cash and complete the task with the help of neighbors, who can fill those building positions or send building permits as gifts, for instance.

Although waiting for neighbors to respond might take a bit longer, being patient saves that hard-earned Cash for stuff that it's truly *needed* for. If you really can't stand waiting, go get some more conscientious neighbors (see Chapter 6).

The same idea applies when buying Energy Batteries with City Cash (see Chapter 4). Sure, it'd be nice to be able to use some more Energy right this second, but if you just wait a few hours, your Energy meter will be full once again. Even better, get some neighbors to send you some extra Energy instead!

✓ **Let your taste guide you:** If you focus strictly on profitability and efficiency, there are only a few items you should even consider spending your City Cash on (see Chapter 12). Of course, such a myopic focus can lead to a very dull city, and some very dull play time for you. If you see a City Cash item that strikes your fancy, for any reason, go ahead and throw down a couple of virtual bucks on it. You only manage a virtual city once, right? It's just fake money! Live a little!

Getting the Goods on Goods

Although you can build your fortune simply by collecting from housing and community buildings, running effective businesses is the key to sending your Coin count into the stratosphere. To do that, you need Goods to supply those businesses, as detailed in Chapter 4.

Storing Goods: Sheds, Silos, and such

Before you can start collecting Goods for your businesses, you need a place to store them. CityVille offers a variety of storage buildings for this purpose, as we outline in Table 7-3.

Table 7-3			Goods Storage Buildings		
Name	**Storage Capacity**	**Cost**	**Storage Per Cost**	**Size**	**Storage Per Size**
Silo	100 Goods	250 Coins	0.4 per Coin	2 x 2 (4 blocks total)	25 per block
Red Barn	415 Goods	1,000 Coins	0.415 per Coin	4 x 4 (16 blocks total)	25.9375 per block
Sticks	485 Goods	1,125 Coins	.431 per Coin	3 x 6 (18 blocks total)	26.94 per block
Cargo Shed	1,000 Goods	20 City Cash	50 per Cash	3 x 3 (9 blocks total)	111.11
Pier	420 Goods	5,000 Coins	0.084 per Coin	1 to 16	20 to 420

As you can see from Table 7-3, larger storage options are slightly more efficient, both on a cost and land-use basis. For this reason, focus on using Sticks exclusively for your Goods storage if at all possible. Sure, you might want to use the occasional Silo if you can't afford a full Sticks, or place a couple of piers and boats to enable some shipping missions (see the "Setting up and scheduling shipping missions" section later in this chapter), but for the most part, stick with the Sticks.

The Cargo Shed is a special case; it's by far the most efficient use of land space for storage, packing four times as many Goods in each block of land than its closest competition. The only downside, of course, is the dear cost in City Cash, which, unlike Coins, is very hard to replace.

Buying and selling Goods using shipping and train missions

Planting and harvesting crops is the simplest way to acquire Goods. But there are some problems with relying on crops for your Goods. They take up precious space in your city. They wither if you don't harvest them promptly. Most importantly, they take up a good deal of your Energy to harvest.

Buying Goods from train or boat missions solves some of these problems, giving you Goods without as much of the hassle. You pay a bit more for the privilege, but the benefits can be well worth it.

Scheduling a train mission

To use your Train Station to buy or sell Goods, you first need at least five neighbors to unlock it. After you do this, follow these steps to complete a train mission.

1. **Click your Train Station.**

   This brings up the Train Schedule dialog box, as shown in Figure 7-6.

   If you currently have a train out, you can't schedule another mission until it returns.

2. **Click the tabs to choose whether you want to buy or sell Goods.**

   Click the left and right arrows to see more train missions. Some missions may need to be unlocked.

3. **Click the Send Train button below the mission you want to choose.**

   Each mission lists the amount of time taken, the number of Goods to be bought or sold, and the number of Coins you'll earn or pay for the mission. This information is also contained in Table 7-4 and Table 7-5, along with an analysis of mission efficiency.

If you chose a train mission that requires friends, a friend selection menu appears.

Figure 7-6: The Train Schedule dialog box.

4. **Select the check box next to the friends you want to buy Goods from or sell Goods to.**

   Select the check box next to each friend's name and then click the Send Gift Invitation button. The train leaves on its mission, and your friends can sell or buy Goods when the train arrives in their city. You can hover your mouse over the Train Station to see exactly how long until the train will return.

5. **When the train returns, click the flashing railroad signal in the goals area.**

   The train comes into the station, along with a message telling you how many Goods you sold or received.

6. **Click the Accept button to complete your mission.**

   Goods or Coin icons pop out of the train, to be collected by clicking as normal.

Table 7-4			Train Missions (Buy Goods)		
Neighbors Required	Goods Earned	Coins Spent	Time	Goods Per Coin	Goods per Hour
0 (Samville)	25	62	5 minutes	0.4	7,200
0 (Charlieville*)	300	1,200	5 minutes	0.25	86,400
3	250	500	4 hours	0.5	1,500
4	350	612	8 hours	0.57	1,050
6	450	675	12 hours	0.67	900
8	550	687	1 day	0.8	550
10	700	700	2 days	1	350

* Charlieville missions are available only after you complete the Get Charlie Breakfast quest (see Chapter 8).

Table 7-5			Train Missions (Sell Goods)		
Neighbors Required	Goods Spent	Coins Earned	Time	Coins Per Good	Coins Per Hour
0 (SamVille)	25	87	5 minutes	3.48	1,044
0 (CharlieVille*)	300	600	5 minutes	2	7,200
3	250	925	4 hours	3.7	231.25
4	350	1,365	8 hours	3.9	170.63
6	450	1,844	12 hours	4.1	153.67
8	550	2,365	1 day	4.3	98.54
10	700	3,150	2 days	4.5	65.63

* CharlieVille missions are available only after you complete the Get Charlie Breakfast quest (see Chapter 8).

Picking the best train missions

So which train missions should you choose? Obviously, it depends on your situation. If you need Goods quickly, without spending any Energy, it's hard to beat the Charlieville train mission, assuming you've unlocked it. This mission might cost a lot of Coins, but it's by far the quickest and simplest way to get 300 Goods into your coffers. Remember, as soon as the train returns, you can send it on another mission and really rack up the Goods.

If time is not of the essence, the ten neighbor train missions gives an almost respectable one-to-one Coins-for-Goods ratio, though the eight-neighbor mission is nearly as good, Coin-wise, in half the time. If you choose one of these long-lead missions, remember you can't use the train at all until it returns.

Selling Goods through the train station usually isn't a good idea — plowing those same Goods into your businesses usually results in a better, quicker Coin return, especially if the businesses are augmented by decorations (see Chapter 9). If you absolutely feel the urge to sell Goods using the train, select the ten-neighbor mission to get the best return on your precious Goods.

Setting up and scheduling shipping missions

After you complete The New Seaport quest (see Chapter 8), you can buy piers and boats for your town. Piers can be placed only on the coastline, as shown in Figure 7-7. This means that most of their massive size extends into otherwise useless water, making them more efficient than they first seem, regarding space. Depending on the shape of the coast and the precise placement of the pier, it can take anywhere from 0 to 16 usable plots of land in its placement.

Figure 7-7: A coastline populated with a couple of piers.

Though the 4-x-4-square Boat House has to exist inside the area of your land expansion (see Chapter 4), the actual pier can extend into darker water that isn't technically part of your city. Use this fact to minimize the land footprint of your pier.

Piers might seem expensive for their rather modest storage capacity, but they have the added advantage of letting you place boats alongside them in the water, as shown in Figure 7-7. These boats let you perform shipping missions as yet another method of collecting Goods.

Here are the two schools of thought regarding optimum placement of piers and boats:

✔ **Jam piers as close to each other as possible,** as shown in Figure 7-8. This has the advantage of maximizing your Goods storage per land use, but you may not be able to keep as many boats because some of the boat positions overlap. This means you can't send as many boat missions at once, as compared to . . .

Figure 7-8: The Pick a Ship Mission menu.

✔ **Spread piers apart** so that each pier can have as many as eight boats along its docks, as shown in Figure 7-7. This maximizes the opportunity to have simultaneous shipping missions going on but can lead to slightly inefficient use of your coastline for Goods-storing piers.

You can move a pier, but first you must remove all the boats from it.

To schedule a shipping mission, you first need to buy a pier and at least one boat. Then follow these steps.

1. Click a free boat.

This brings up the Pick a Ship Mission menu, as shown in Figure 7-8.

You can also find this menu by clicking the Shipping tab on the Build menu.

Click the left and right arrows on this menu to see more options. Hover your mouse over any option to see that mission's name, its return in Goods, and the amount of time it will take. This information is also contained in Table 7-6.

2. **Click the shipping mission you want to undertake.**

   If you got to the shipping menu through the Build menu, you have to click a boat to use for the mission. The ship sails off into the ocean, leaving a pale outline and a buoy in its place. You can then click more boats to send them on the same mission

   If you want to select a different mission for another boat, click the red circle with a slash through it in the Tools menu in the bottom-right corner of the play area.

3. **Wait for the boat to return with Goods and then click it to unload them.**

   Goods icons fall out of the boat. You can click these icons to collect them, as normal. Unloading a ship takes 1 Energy from your meter.

Table 7-6	Shipping Missions					
Name	**Unlock Requirements**	**Goods**	**Coins**	**Time**	**Goods Per Coin**	**Goods Per Hour**
San Francisco Supply	None	19	25	5 minutes	0.76	228
Sydney Sails	None	87	70	8 hours	1.24	10.88
Paris Parcels	None	137	95	1 day	1.44	5.7
Shanghai Shipping	6 neighbors	38	44	1 hour	0.86	38
London Liners	8 neighbors	56	55	4 hours	1.02	14
Dubai Direct	9 neighbors	100	76	12 hours	1.32	8.33
New York Novelties	10 neighbors	112	79	18 hours	1.42	6.22
Rio Routes	12 neighbors	162	109	2.1 days	1.49	3.21
Rome Relics	15 neighbors	194	131	3.1 days	1.48	2.61
Caribbean Cargo	Complete Lost Rusty goals (see Chapter 8)	101	146	1.6 days	0.69	2.63

Picking the best shipping missions

The first thing that jumps out about shipping missions from Table 7-6 is that they're much more expensive than comparable crop harvests, on a purely Coin-based perspective. The very best shipping missions don't even compare to some of the worst crops, on a pure Goods-per-Coin basis.

This Coin inefficiency isn't as big a deal as it seems at first, though, when you consider how many more Goods you get for your Energy and time using shipping. Compare the Rome Relics shipping mission to planting a plot of peas, for instance. Both take 3.1 days and 1 Energy to complete, but the shipping mission leaves you with 39 extra Goods to show for your trouble.

These Goods-per-hour and Goods-per-Energy benefits are constant across all shipping missions and can really add up after a few. Relying on ships for your Goods also frees up precious farmland, which can be put to more productive pursuits than the useless ocean.

Managing Your Energy

Any real world mayor will tell you there just aren't enough hours in a day to do everything you want to do in managing a bustling metropolis. In CityVille, this limitation is simulated by an Energy system that limits the number of productive tasks you can undertake before you have to stop playing for a while.

Besides forcing you to prioritize which actions are most important to your city, this Energy system also forces you to take a break from non-stop CityVille tending. This can be a very good thing — without the Energy system, a few CityVille addicts would never stop playing!

Getting Energy

As one of the most important resources in the game, it's important to know all the ways you can gain Energy. Here they are:

- **Automatic refills over time:** This is the most common way of obtaining more Energy. After you use some Energy from your meter, you see a small countdown timer above the Energy meter, as shown in Figure 7-9. This meter tells you exactly how much longer you have to wait before getting one more Energy. After the timer finishes, if your Energy still isn't full, the countdown immediately starts again and you're on your way to yet another Energy!

- **Leveling up:** Every time you obtain a new level (see the "Earning Experience Points and Levels" section later in the chapter), you gain Energy equal to your Reputation level (see Chapter 6). Keep an eye on your Experience Points meter to know when this Energy boost is coming, and be sure to visit friends frequently to increase your Reputation level and ensure you take full advantage of this bonus.

Figure 7-9: The countdown timer for more Energy.

✔ **Battery items:** Batteries are one of the most important items your neighbors can send to you. Found in +1, +2, and +3 Energy varieties, these items stay in your inventory until you're ready to use them to refill your Energy meter. (For more on the inventory, see Chapter 3.) You can also purchase larger Energy Batteries from the Build menu using City Cash (see Chapter 4), but the prices make this method prohibitively expensive.

One of the best ways to get more Energy Batteries is by sending them to your neighbors. Remember, it just takes them a single click to send one back.

✔ **Energy drops:** When you collect from buildings, you sometimes see Lightning Bolt icons pop out along with the usual Coins, Goods, and collectables. Click these icons to add 1 Energy to your meter.

Community buildings and franchises supplied by neighbors tend to be the most likely buildings to drop these Energy icons when you collect from them, making this collection an Energy-free proposition. In some cases, these buildings will actually drop *2* Energy icons when you collect, which means you actually *gain* Energy when you collect from them. Don't that beat all?

Using Energy

So now that you have your Energy, what can you do with it? We're glad you asked. Here's a complete list of the actions in CityVille that require you to have at least 1 Energy in your meter. Unless otherwise noted, each action takes 1 Energy:

- Collecting from housing, businesses, and community buildings

- Harvesting one plot of crops

- Removing Goods from a boat

- Removing a tree from your city

- Erecting a building (exact Energy needed to complete the building varies)

Out of Energy for the time being? Don't fret; there's plenty of stuff that you can do without spending Energy:

- Supply businesses with Goods.

- Supply franchises through your headquarters (HQ).

- Plant crops.

- Start a train or shipping mission.

- Start a new building (but you need to spend Energy to complete the building).

- Help neighbors (the 5 Energy you can use helping each neighbor doesn't impact your primary Energy meter).

- Place decorations.

- Expand your city.

- Rearrange buildings and decorations.

For more on how to best make use of your Energy, see Chapter 9.

Earning Experience Points and Levels

Although currency, Goods, and Energy are all important measurements of your progress in the game, your access to these resources can bounce up and down as you go through different points in the earning and spending cycle. If you're looking for a resource that measures your CityVille progress in a strictly upward direction, Experience Points are your ticket.

Finding out about Experience Points

Experience Points are represented by a blue Star icon that emerges when you perform certain in-game actions, such as

- Collecting rent from a building

- Harvesting a crop

- Unloading Goods from a boat

✔ Chopping down a tree

✔ Performing a build step on a new building

✔ Visiting a neighbor (with some limits, see Chapter 6 for specifics)

✔ Clicking certain bonus links on your Facebook Wall (see Chapter 6)

Just like Coins, Goods, and collectables, you can collect these Experience Point icons by clicking them. Occasionally one of these actions will create a Double-Star icon, worth two Experience Points!

You can see the total number of Experience Points you've earned so far in the meter in the upper-right corner of the play area.

Unlocking new items by earning levels

In CityVille, *levels* are simply a way of acknowledging that you're reached a certain Experience Point milestone. When you reach a new level, you earn a one-time Energy bonus equal to your current Reputation level (see Chapter 6).

Sometimes, unlocking a new level also means unlocking new items for purchase in the Build menu, as we outline in Table 7-7. Up through Level 28, earning new levels can also increase the maximum amount of Energy you can store in your meter at one time. Each level also comes with a new nickname for your town (see Table 7-7).

Table 7-7		CityVille Levels		
Level	Name	Experience Points Needed	Maximum Energy	Items Unlocked
1	Dot on a Map	0	12	N/A
2	Crossroads	4	13	Carrots
3	One-Horse Town	16	14	Country Home
4	Two-Horse Town	31	15	Suburban House, Post Office
5	Smallishville	78	16	Loft Apartments
6	Teeny Town	125	17	Eggplant
7	Tween Town	175	18	Police Station
8	Young Town	219	19	Red Barn

(continued)

Table 7-7 (continued)

Level	Name	Experience Points Needed	Maximum Energy	Items Unlocked
9	LargerVille	276	20	Watermelon, Emergency Clinic
10	Coup de Ville	343	21	N/A
11	Traffic Town	420	21	N/A
12	Big Town	507	22	N/A
13	Terrific Town	604	22	N/A
14	Boom Town	711	23	N/A
15	Wee Lil' City	828	23	Pumpkins, Museum
16	Small City	955	24	N/A
17	Pretty City	1,092	24	N/A
18	Citified City	1,239	25	N/A
19	Happy Hood	1,396	25	N/A
20	Synchronicity	1,563	26	Wheat, Library
21	Silver City	1,740	26	N/A
22	Backwater Burgh	1,927	27	N/A
23	Windy City	2,124	27	N/A
24	Vast Village	2,331	28	N/A
25	Happy Hamlet	2,548	28	Upscale Condos, Peas
26	Shining Shire	2,775	29	N/A
27	City Scape	3,003	29	N/A
28	Funkadelphia	3,232	30	N/A
29	Modest Municipality	3,462	30	N/A
30	Booming Burgh	3,693	30	N/A
31	Witty City	3,925	30	N/A
32	Urban E Anse	4,158	30	Middle School
33	Slick Suburb	4,392	30	N/A
34	Perfect Principality	4,627	30	
35	Surging City	4,863	30	Hotel Suites, Firehouse

Level	Name	Experience Points Needed	Maximum Energy	Items Unlocked
36	City Without Pity	5,100	30	N/A
37	Pot-Holed Pit Stop	5,338	30	N/A
38	Stop Light Suburb	5,577	30	N/A
39	Swell City	5,817	30	N/A
40	Port of Progress	6,058	30	Sprawling Mansion, High School
41	Slick City	6,300	30	N/A
42	Capitol City	6,543	30	N/A
43	Peppy Populous	6,787	30	N/A
44	Bustling Borough	7,032	30	N/A
45	Capitol of Cool	7,278	30	Hospital
46	Virtuous Village	7,525	30	N/A
47	Quaint Escape	7,773	30	N/A
48	Concrete Jungle	8,022	30	N/A
49	Popular Province	8,272	30	N/A
50	Rural Retreat	8,523	30	N/A
51	Metropolis	8,874	30	N/A
52	Hoppin' Hood	9,325	30	N/A
53	Emerald City	9,816	30	N/A
54	Neighborly Neighborhood	10,527	30	N/A
55	Breezy City	11,278	30	Chic Boutique, Court House
56	Peppy Podville	12,129	30	N/A
57	Diamond Den	13,080	30	N/A
58	Punctual Prefect	14,131	30	N/A
59	Quaint Quahog	15,282	30	N/A

(continued)

Table 7-7 *(continued)*

Level	Name	Experience Points Needed	Maximum Energy	Items Unlocked
60	Golden Goodsville	16,533	30	Jewelry Store, Modern Art Gallery
61	Great Gotham	17,884	30	N/A
62	Expansive Expo	19,335	30	N/A
63	Country County	20,886	30	N/A
64	County Capitol	22,537	30	N/A
65	Viva Las City	24,288	30	N/A
66	M.C. Master City	26,139	30	N/A
67	City-O-Rama	28,090	30	N/A
68	Citinator	30,141	30	N/A
69	Double Duchy	32,292	30	N/A
70	Crafty Commonwealth	34,543	30	N/A
71	Popping Province	36,894	30	N/A
72	Laudable Land	39,345	30	N/A
73	Radical Region	41,896	30	N/A
74	Fantastic Bailiwick	44,547	30	N/A
75	Super Metropolis	47,298	30	N/A
76	Captivating Canton	50,149	30	
77	City Shipper	53,100	30	N/A
78	City o' Lights	56,151	30	N/A
79	Happy Valley	59,302	30	N/A
80	Groove Town	62,553	30	N/A

After you reach Level 80, you continue to earn Experience Points, but you don't earn a new level.

Those extra Experience Points might not be useless forever. Zynga sometimes increases the level cap.

Earning Experience Points quickly

Can't wait to get your level up higher than those of your neighbors? Here are some strategies to turbo-charge your leveling:

✓ **Focus on quick turnaround buildings and crops:** Remember, you get the same Experience Points from every building and crop, whether it took a few minutes or a few days to be ready for your click.

Focus on buildings like the Country Home and Bakery, crops like strawberries, and shipping missions like San Francisco Supply. Each of these can be ready to generate Experience Points in just five minutes or less. See Chapter 4 for a complete list of buildings that generate Experience Points quickly.

Of course, all this constant clicking uses up a lot of Energy, and might earn you less money than other buildings, but this isn't as big a concern early on, when the new levels are tightly packed together and available buildings cost less money.

Earning new levels comes with an Energy bonus, which can quickly lead to more clicks and more experience and more levels and more Energy bonuses!

✓ **Visit neighbors frequently:** Not only does visiting neighbors get you a free Experience Point, it also earns an Energy point that you can use in your own city to earn further Experience Points. New neighbors are even better, offering 3 Energy points in addition to the standard Experience Point.

Build up that Reputation level, too, so you can earn more Energy bonuses for new levels and get bonuses for helping as many neighbors as possible (see Chapter 6 for more on Reputation levels and helping neighbors).

✓ **Build lots of community buildings:** True, community buildings only produce Experience Points once every 24 hours, making them one of the slower methods of earning experience. However, clicking community buildings almost always produces at least 1 Energy point, making the experience (and Coins) they produce essentially free! Sometimes they even produce two Energy bolts, meaning you're gaining Energy with every click. If you have the space (and the money, and willing neighbors to staff the buildings), filling your city with cheap City Halls and Post Offices can be a great way to supercharge your daily experience haul.

✓ **Maximize your Energy use:** Because practically every action that takes Energy produces experience, getting more Energy leads pretty directly to more experience. See Chapter 9 for more on maximizing your Energy use.

Managing Other Inventory Items

Most resources in CityVille are nebulous concepts, measured in meters and counters that hover ever-present over the top of your play area. And then there are the resources discussed in this section. These get hidden away in your My Stuff menu after they're collected, to be used at a later date.

Collecting collectables

Collectables are a special class of resources that are useless on their own, but useful in conjunction with other collectables in that same collection set. Collectables pop up randomly when collecting rent from buildings or harvesting crops. Which type of collectable you get depends on the specific building or crop you click, as shown in Table 7-8.

Table 7-8	Collections and Collectables	
Collection Name	**Collectables Found by Collecting/ Harvesting From**	**Reward for Trade In**
Peaceful Living	Cozy Cottage, Country Home, and Lake House	White Picket Fence
Suburbia	Family Townhouse and Suburban House	Red Dog House
Main Street	Loft Apartments and Stylish Contemporary	50 Coins and 3 XP
City Life	Terraced Brownstone and Apartment Complex	50 Coins and 3 XP
Rural	Ranch House, Newlywed House, and Rita's Country Home	25 Goods and 3 XP
High Society	Modern Chateau, Colonial Chalet, and Sprawling Mansion	Driveway Gate
Down Town	Upscale Condos and Hotel Suites	Tavern
Jet Setter	Skyscraper Condos, Glass Condos, Atrium Lofts, and Penthouse Tower	Tuxedo Rental
Just Desserts	Rent from Bakery	50 Coins and 3 XP
Garden	Rent from Flower Kiosk	Purple Flowers
Early Riser	Rent from Coffee Shop and Hot Cocoa Shop	50 Goods and 3 Energy
Game	Rent from Toy Store and Video Game Store	50 Coins and 3 Energy
Fast Food	Burger Joint	Gray Hen
Comfort Food	Diner	Hot Dog Cart

Collection Name	Collectables Found by Collecting/ Harvesting From	Reward for Trade In
Forever Young	Cosmetic Store	Pink Flowers
Watering Hole	Pool Hall and Tavern	3 Energy and 3 XP
Fitness	Bike Shop	50 Coins and 3 XP
Designer	Shoe Store, Handbag Store, and Sunglasses Store	50 Coins and 3 XP
French Cuisine	French Restaurant	Bird Fountain
Surf and Turf	Seafood Restaurant and Tower Eats	Black Cow
Asian Cuisine	Sushi Bar	Japanese Maple Tree
Bridal	Wedding Store and Tuxedo Rental	Newlywed House
Silver Screen	Cinema	Highway Billboard
Convenience Store	Corner Store	3 Energy and 3 XP
Perfect Fit	Chic Boutique and Laundromat	50 Coins and 25 Goods
Home Furnishings	Furniture Store	3,000 Coins
Home Entertainment	Music Store	3,000 Coins
Houseware	Appliance Store	50 Coins and 25 Goods
Bling	Jewelry Store	3,000 Coins
Bookworm	Bookstore	50 Coins and 3 XP
Lunar New Year	Noodle Shop, City Dojo, and Fireworks Shop	Country Pagoda
Corn	Corn	White Goat
Strawberry	Strawberries	50 Coins and 3 XP
Watermelon	Watermelon	25 Goods and 3 XP
Pumpkin	Pumpkins	3 Energy and 3 XP
Carrot	Carrots	Gray Bunny
Wheat	Wheat	White Chicken
Eggplant	Eggplant	50 Coins and 3 XP
Pea	Peas	Corner Store
Cranberry	Cranberries	50 Coins and 3 Energy

Each collection is made up of five distinct collectibles that vary by collection. The Peaceful Living collection, for instance, is made up of an EZ Chair, Folding Table, Garden Gnome, Bird House, and Radio. There's no functional difference between the different collectibles in each collection, save for the image and name, and which specific collectable you get from your clicking is totally random. This means you may sometimes get dozens of a collectable before you find a single instance of another collectable in that same set. Although this can be frustrating, especially if you're trying to complete a quest — just keep at it. Eventually the law of averages means you will complete your collection.

After you collect one of each collectable in a certain set, you can collect a reward by turning in the complete set. To do this, follow these steps:

1. **Choose My Stuff⇨Collections.**

   The My Stuff menu button is an image of a present and a box in the lower-right corner of the play area. The Collections dialog box appears, as shown in Figure 7-10. The number of each collectable you have is shown as a small number accompanying each collectable icon in this menu. If you currently have none of a collectable, that icon appears grayed out.

Figure 7-10: The Collections dialog box.

2. **Scroll through the list of collections by clicking the left and right arrows, and then click the green Trade In button next to any complete collection.**

The Trade In button is grayed out if you don't have all five items in a given collection.

Click the Trade In button trade only in one set of that collection, even if you have multiple complete sets. You can click the Trade In button again to trade in further sets.

The reward is added to your inventory and a dialog box offers to post a message to your Facebook Wall.

You can click the Share Coins button to post a Coin bonus to your Facebook Wall (see Chapter 6).

Taking inventory: Permits, seals, and such

The vast majority of items and resources in the game are placed in your city immediately or reside in special meters that keep track of how much you have at any one moment. Inventory items are different. These items sit in your inventory until you actively use them or place them in your city.

Only certain types of items can reside in your inventory, including

- ✔ Items sent to your by neighbors (See Chapter 6)
- ✔ Items collected as rewards from trading in collections
- ✔ Items collected as rewards for leveling up
- ✔ Items collected as rewards for completing goals
- ✔ Items introduced as new features in the game after you start playing

To use items in your inventory, follow these steps:

1. **Choose My Stuff⟳Inventory.**

   The My Stuff menu button is an image of a present and a box in the lower-right corner of the play area. The Inventory dialog box appears, as shown in Figure 7-11. The number of each item you have is shown as a small white number accompanying each item's icon. Click the left and right arrows, if available, to see more items in your inventory.

2. **Click the center of the item you want to use.**

   Not all items can be used by clicking them:

   - Items with a blue and white starburst pattern in the background — such as zoning permits, city seals, and building grants — are used for building construction and city expansion. See Chapter 4 for more on constructing buildings with these inventory items.

   - Items used for collection-based quests — such as snowflakes and mittens — reside in your inventory until they're needed for quest completion. See Chapter 8 for more on quests.

Figure 7-11: The Inventory dialog box.

If you clicked an Energy Battery, that Battery's Energy is added to your meter automatically. You can stop here. If you didn't click a Battery, the item appears under your cursor for placement in your city, move on to Step 3.

3. **Place the decoration or building as normal.**

See Chapter 3 for more on placing items in your city. If you change your mind about placing the item, simply click the red circle with a slash through it in the bottom-right corner of the play area. The item returns to your inventory.

You can click the big red X button next to any item to remove that item from your inventory. A confirmation menu asks how many of the item you want to remove; choose the quantity using the plus and minus buttons and then click the Remove button to confirm the removal. The only real reason to do this is if you're approaching the in-game limit of 2,000 items in your inventory. How the heck did you get so many inventory items?

Using wish lists to get the items you want

Hoping and praying the right collectable or inventory item will simply fall into your lap is not a very effective game play strategy. Putting those items on a wish list tends to be much more effective, especially if you have conscientious neighbors.

Here's how to add items to your wish list:

1. **Choose My Stuff⇨Collections (or Inventory).**

   The My Stuff menu button is an image of a present and a box in the lower-right corner of the play area. The Collections (or Inventory) dialog box appears, as shown in Figures 7-10 and 7-11, respectively.

2. **Click the small Paper icon with a green plus sign in the bottom-left corner of the item you want to add to the wish list.**

   Not all inventory items will include this icon. Only items used as building materials (see Chapter 6) or to complete collection-based quests can be added to a wish list.

   The item appears in the wish list area at the top of the menu, as shown in Figure 7-12.

   You can have only five distinct items in your wish list at any one time, and you share one wish list between your inventory and collectables.

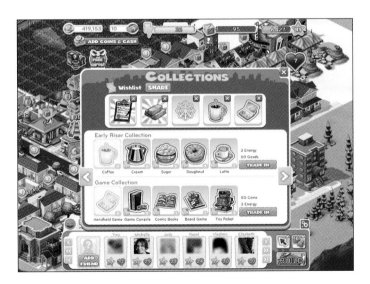

Figure 7-12: A wish list full of collectables and inventory items.

3. **Click the green Share button to post a note about your wish list to your Facebook Wall.**

   This note includes details about your wish list and encourages neighbors to click through to help you by sending items from it. Even if you don't post the wish list to your Wall, neighbors can give you wish list items through the My Neighbors menu (see Chapter 6).

Completing Quests

*U*nlike most modern video games, CityVille doesn't technically have an ending. Instead of working toward a well-defined end point, you can keep expanding your city until the end of time (or until the publisher Zynga goes out of business — whichever comes first). With CityVille, simply managing your own town is its own reward.

Of course, that doesn't mean the game is directionless. Although nothing stops you from maintaining a humble little hamlet with only a few buildings, most players naturally strive for self-imposed quests like collecting more money, expanding their city's population, establishing more businesses, and reaching the next in-game level. CityVille gently encourages quests like these by unlocking new items and providing other benefits to diligent city managers as they earn more money and reach new levels.

If you aren't satisfied just puttering around town, though, CityVille also includes a more explicit structure of enumerated quests. By asking players to perform specific tasks in a certain order, these quests do double duty — teaching players about new facets of the game and giving an optional set structure to your vast array of city building options. Completing quests also earns relatively minor in-game rewards, including access to some rather important in-game items.

In this chapter, we introduce you to the basics of CityVille's quest system, give you some general tips on completing quests, and then walk you through the branching path of unlockable quests that leads you to the mayorship and beyond.

Figuring Out How Quests Work

Before you participate in CityVille's quest system, you have to know what the game expects of you. This section walks you through how you know what quests are available and how to choose which quests to tackle in which order.

Viewing quests and requirements

Avoiding the CityVille quest system is pretty difficult. As soon as you build your first house, a Welcome to Your Town icon appears in the tasks area on the left side of the play area, signifying your very first quest. As shown in Figure 8-1, the game calls your attention to this icon with a huge, bouncing Click Me banner.

Figure 8-1: Your first quest, and the somewhat obnoxious arrow that calls it to your attention.

Click the icon to bring up your first quest — naming your town. Type your desired town name in the box that appears and click Okay.

Wasn't that simple? You've now completed your first quest. You can click the Share Coins button to post a Coin bonus to your Facebook Wall, as we discuss in Chapter 6. The Welcome to Your Town icon is replaced by a Newspaper icon, which you can click to see an animated newspaper announcing your town's name (as if you didn't already know).

Unfortunately, not every quest is that simple to complete. In fact, right after you name your town, a House icon for the game's first complex quest appears in the tasks area. Click the icon to bring up a welcome message from one of the game's characters, as shown in Figure 8-2. Click Okay to bring up the requirements menu for the quest, as shown in Figure 8-3.

Figure 8-2: A quest welcome message.

Figure 8-3: A quest requirements menu.

You can bring up the requirements menu again simply by clicking the Quest icon on the left side of the screen — no need to go through the welcome message again.

Each quest is made up of a series of quantifiable tasks that need to be performed to complete the quest. As you can see in Figure 8-3, the requirements menu here includes

- **The quest's title.**
- **The tasks you must complete for this quest.**

  In this case, the tasks are

  - *Harvest four crops*
  - *Plant four crops*

- **A fraction that represents your current progress toward each requirement:**

  - *The left number* show how many times you've done the task.
  - *The right number* is the number of times you need to do the task to complete the requirement.

  When an individual requirement is complete, those numbers are replaced with a green check mark.

- **Hints from one of CityVille's stable of characters for how to complete the quest (no matter how simple that quest might actually be).**

Click the Okay button or the X in the corner of the requirements menu to return to the play area.

Don't worry about keeping track of these requirements yourself; the game will make sure to note any actions you take toward requirements on all your active quests. Early in the game, in fact, it sometimes uses large yellows arrows to point out exactly what you need to click to complete the quest. Regardless, the game constantly monitors your progress, so don't worry about checking in with your progress.

Using the All Quests Notebook

As you amass more and more active quests at a time, the icons for these quests may overflow your tasks area. When this happens, the overflow quests are sent to your All Quests Notebook, as represented by the tiny Notebook icon with a CV on the front on the left side of the play area.

Click the Quest Notebook to bring up the All Quests menu, as shown in Figure 8-4.

Figure 8-4: The All Quests menu, with the mouse hovering over one of the quest icons.

✓ **Hovering over an icon in this menu shows you**

- *Your progress toward each of its requirements.*

- *The eventual rewards for completing the quest.*

   This is the only way to view that reward information before completing the quest.

✓ **Clicking a Quest icon in this menu sends it to the main tasks area, where it can be clicked for quick access to the requirements.**

   The quest currently at the bottom of the tasks area cycles into the notebook when you do this.

✓ **When you're done, click the X button in the upper-right corner of the All Quests menu to return to the game.**

Spending and cajoling your way through quest requirements

Completing quests in CityVille requires focus and the determination to follow through. Or, if you have deep pockets, it can sometimes mean spending some City Cash.

Chapter 7 shows how to earn or buy City Cash.

As shown in Figure 8-5, some quest requirements feature a *City Cash* to Finish button, with a specific cost for skipping that requirement (in this example, a 45 to Finish button). To spend your way out of a tricky requirement, simply click the button and then click Yes on the confirmation that appears.

Figure 8-5: Click the 45 to Finish button to spend your way through some tricky requirements.

If you have a good number of attentive neighbors playing the game (you really should — see Chapter 6 for more on why), getting the items needed for the requirement you're skipping is probably just a matter of patience and gentle cajoling. In fact, as you can see in Figure 8-5, there's also a big Ask Your Friends button allowing you to post a cajoling note straight to your Facebook Wall, as we discuss in Chapter 4 (if you've recently asked your friends for help with that requirement, this button isn't active).

Usually, spending City Cash to get through a quest isn't worth it. City Cash doesn't come easily; if you waste it, you'll likely have to spend some real money to get more. (See Chapter 7 for more on managing your City Cash.) The reward for the quest probably isn't worth so dear a price, whatever it is. Then again, if you've had a particularly tricky quest sitting in your tasks area for weeks and you just can't seem to get any of your friends to send you those last few items, no matter how much you beg, and you simply can't bear to see that Snowflake icon staring back at you for *one more second,* by all means, shell out the City Cash.

Completing quests and unlocking new ones

If a quest has multiple requirements for completion, the game notifies you of your progress with a big Progress arrow pointing to the Quest icon when you complete a requirement.

When you've completed all the requirements, a Goal Complete notification appears, as shown in Figure 8-6. This notification tells you what bonus you've received, what items you've unlocked, and tips about the game (sort of like this book!)

Figure 8-6: A Goal Complete notification.

Each completed quest also comes with a Share Your Goods button allowing you to post a bonus to your Wall. This bonus includes Coins, Experience Points, or Goods that can be collected by your neighbors, as we discuss in Chapter 6. If you'd rather skip the notification, click the X in the upper-right corner.

Sometimes you can complete the requirements for a quest only after you unlock it.

When you complete a quest, at least one new Quest icon appears in the tasks area to replace it. Clearing out current quests is usually the only way to get new ones to appear, so be sure to complete quests as quickly as possible to bring up new tasks (and new potential rewards). See the following section in this chapter for more information about which goals are unlocked when.

The Path to Mayorship (and Beyond!)

Quests in CityVille don't appear at random. The game's designers have constructed a set path through increasingly difficult quests, each of which appears only after the one before it is completed. The path contains many branches, but contains a strong, straight root system that starts with your first neighborhood and ends with giant skyscrapers towering over your metropolis!

Consider this section your roadmap through these branching quest paths. Instead of wondering what you have to do next, you can use this section to see what quests will be unlocked soon, and prepare yourself and your city for what's coming. If you're really good, you might even be able to complete a quest as soon as you click its icon to see its requirements. It's like you can see into the future!

Prioritizing quests

After you've played the game for a while, chances are your tasks area will overflow with more quests than you know what to do with. Some players like to ignore these quests as much as possible and to simply let the requirements complete themselves by happenstance as they play the game. There's nothing wrong with this style of play. But if you want to work through your quests list in an efficient manner, you have to prioritize which quests are most important.

You can find the most important quests to complete in the "Working through the primary quests" section later in the chapter. Consider these quests the trunk of the constantly branching quest tree, where the most lucrative unlockable items can be found. Focusing on this path also ensures that you gradually open all the other branching paths the game throws at you, as we list in the "Meandering down the quest branches" section, later in this chapter.

Follow these guidelines to prioritize your quest completion effectively:

- **Focus on one quest, or a small number, instead of spreading yourself over many quests at once.** You're best off focusing your limited Energy on one requirement and doing everything you can to complete that requirement before moving on to the next one.

  Of course, you can work on a second quest while you're waiting for factors outside your control on the first. If you've put out a request for items for a quest that requires donations from your neighbors, for instance, you can safely put that quest to the side and work on another.

⯈ **Clear out the simple, cheap quests first and then move on.** Not only do you get the reward for completing a quest but another quest also cycles into your list, leading to potentially more rewards

The difficult, expensive quest will still be there later, when all the easy quests are done.

The rest of this chapter shows the requirements for unlocking and completing specific quests.

Working through the primary quests

The quests we list in Table 8-1 form one long, unbroken chain that guides you from a barely functioning town to a towering metropolis! The quests are listed in the order they're unlocked, meaning completing one quest brings up the one below it. Certain quests also bring up a secondary, branching quest, as listed in the Branching Quests column. For information on these quests, see the "Meandering down the quest branches" section, later in the chapter.

The Rewards column shows what items you receive for completing each quest, with important, unlocked items listed in bold. See Chapter 4 for more on all these items.

Be careful when completing quests that grant Energy points or Goods — if you don't have the capacity to hold these rewards when they are earned, they'll be effectively wasted. See Chapter 7 for more on storing Goods.

Table 8-1	Main Quest Path		
Quest	*Tasks*	*Rewards*	*Branching Quests*
First Neighborhood	Increase population to 50 Place two asphalt roads	50 Coins	Farmin' with Rita (see Table 8-3)
Build a Bakery	Buy a bakery Supply a Bakery with Goods Collect from a Bakery	25 Goods	The Pastry Tour (see Table 8-4)
Plant a City Flag	Place a city flag	**Build City Hall quest unlocked**	Open New Businesses (see Table 8-2)
Build City Hall	Build a City Hall	2 Experience Points	
Clear Trees	Clear three Wild Trees	100 Coins	Find Hidden Key (see Table 8-5)

(continued)

Table 8-1 *(continued)*

Quest	Tasks	Rewards	Branching Quests
Rita's Flower Garden	Place six Shade Trees Place two Pink Flowers Place eight Blue Flowers	50 Goods	
The Burger Joint	Build a Burger Joint	**Chateau unlocked**	Build Edgar's Chateau (see Table 8-2)
Build a Silo	Place two Storage Silos	100 Coins	Scout Train Routes (see Table 8-6)
Build Franchises	Visit City Sam Place a franchise in Samantha's City	50 Goods	
Build Headquarters	Build a HQ building	50 Goods	
Run Remote Franchises	Click your HQ and then click Supply	100 Coins	Expand Franchise (see Table 8-7)
Fuel Town Finances	Collect from businesses ten times Collect from residences ten times Reach a population of 250	2 Energy	Expansive Thinking (see Table 8-2)
Build a New Park	Place an Arboretum Place three decorations	50 Goods	Place Picnic Tables (see Table 8-8)
Increase Population	Reach a population of 500 Collect from businesses 50 times	**Grade School unlocked**	Helpin' Rita (see Table 8-9)
Build School	Place a Grade School Finish a Grade School	**Playground unlocked**	Build a Playground (see Table 8-10)
Become Mayor	Have a population of 1,000 Collect from businesses 30 times	Zoning permit	
The New Seaport	Have three expansions Lay three roads	**Pier unlocked**	
Set Sail	Build one pier Build one boat	100 Goods	Captain's Trip (see Table 8-11)
Run Franchise	Supply franchise five times Collect from businesses 25 times	**Cinema unlocked**	Cinema Investment (see Table 8-12)
Grow Population	Have a population of 1,500 Have six expansions	10 Energy	Little Italy (see Table 8-13)

Quest	Tasks	Rewards	Branching Quests
Central Park	Place 12 decorations	200 Coins	Picnic Tables (see Table 8-14)
State Fair Pitch	Collect from businesses 30 times Collect from houses 30 times	**Expo Tent unlocked**	Restaurant Research (see Table 8-15)
Animal Gifts	Have an Expo Tent decoration Have two Gray Hens Have one White Chicken	**Carousel unlocked**	State Fair Snacks (see Table 8-2)
Fair Carousel	Have a Carousel Community Building Have 2,500 population	200 Coins	
Build City Funds	Collect from businesses 50 times Collect from houses 50 times Ask friends for eight capital endorsements (or spend 10 City Cash to skip)	**Batting Cage unlocked**	Sports Team (see Table 8-2)
Feed the Fans	Collect two hot dogs Collect two sodas	**Baseball Field unlocked**	
Build and Recruit	Have a Stadium Have a population of 4,000	100 Goods	
New Fire Station	Have a Fire Station in your city Collect from the Fire Station Collect 12 fire axes (or spend 60 City Cash to skip)	200 Coins	Supply Capital City (see Table 8-16)
Hungry Firemen	Have three eggs and toast collectibles (collected from diners) Have three bacon collect-ibles (collected from diners) Have three grits by harvest-ing corn	100 Goods	
Smoke Signal	Collect rent 15 times Collect neighbor rent 15 times	2 Experience Points	

(continued)

Table 8-1 *(continued)*

Quest	Tasks	Rewards	Branching Quests
Build a Hospital	Have a Hospital in your city Collect from the Hospital three times	**Capitol Building unlocked**	
Community Checkup	Reach a population of 5,000 Collect from community buildings ten times Have a State Capitol building in your city	200 Coins	
The Doctor Is In	Have three comic book collectibles (collected from Toy or Video Game Stores) Collect from a Toy Store five times	100 Goods	
Doctor's Toys	Collect from a Video Game Store five times Collect three Robot Toy collectibles (collected from Toy or Video Game Stores)	2 Energy	
First Date Place	Have a Sushi Bar in your city Have a Cinema in your city Have two movie ticket collectibles (collected from Cinemas)	200 Coins	
Chocolate and Roses	Have six rose collectibles (collected from Flower Shops) Collect 12 boxed chocolates from friends (spend 60 City Cash to skip)	2 Experience Points	
Dress for Date	Have one hairbrush collectible (collected from Cosmetic Stores) Have two high heel collectibles (collected from Shoe, Sunglasses, and Handbag Stores) Collect from the Elementary School three times	100 Goods	The Date Is On (see Table 8-17)
Capital Business	Have three Mansions Have three Hotel Suites	200 Coins	

Quest	Tasks	Rewards	Branching Quests
Get Rich Rent	Collect rent from Mansions ten times Collect rent from Hotel Suites ten times	100 Goods	
Collect a Million	Have 1,000,000 Coins	**Mint unlocked**	
Mint Your Success	Have a Mint place in your city Have two Skyscraper Apartments	2 Energy	

Meandering down the quest branches

While marching like a soldier down the main quest path to unlock the coveted Mint might be efficient, it can get tired pretty quickly. Sometimes, another goal will catch your eye and strike your fancy, taking you down a pleasing diversion before leaving you with your more important work.

These are those quests.

Simple secondary quests

Some simple quests are allowed after you complete certain quests we list in Table 8-1. Table 8-2 lists quests that you can perform with a minimal number of tasks. They're a quick way to bag some rewards and build your resources.

Table 8-2		Simple Secondary Quests	
Quest	**Required Quest**	**Tasks**	**Reward**
Open New Businesses	Plant a City Flag	Build a Toy Store	25 Goods
Build Edgar's Chateau	The Burger Joint	Have a Chateau Place six decorations	100 Coins
Scout Businesses	Build Edgar's Chateau	Send ten Tour Buses	1 Experience Point
Expansive Thinking	Fuel Town Finances	Have one expansion	50 Goods

(continued)

Table 8-2 *(continued)*

Quest	Required Quest	Tasks	Reward
State Fair Snacks	Animal Gifts	Have one strawberry jam by harvesting strawberries Have one corn on the cob by harvesting corn Have one baby carrot by harvesting carrots	2 Energy
Sports Team	Build City Funds	Have one Batting Cage Have four Colonial Chalets Collect rent from Colonial Chalets 16 times	200 Goods

Complex secondary quests

Some of the secondary quests require completion of multiple tasks. Each of these tasks has a separate reward.

Before you can pursue each of the following quests, you must complete a quest that's listed in Table 8-1:

- **Farmin' with Rita:** See Table 8-3; requires First Neighborhood
- **The Pastry Tour:** See Table 8-4; requires Build a Bakery
- **Find Hidden Key:** See Table 8-5; requires Clear Trees
- **Scout Train Routes:** See Table 8-6; requires Build a Silo
- **Expand Franchise:** See Table 8-7; requires Run Remote Franchises
- **Place Picnic Tables:** See Table 8-8; requires Build a New Park
- **Helpin' Rita:** See Table 8-9; requires Increase Population
- **Build a Playground:** See Table 8-10; requires Build School
- **Captain's Trip:** See Table 8-11; requires Set Sail
- **Cinema Investment:** See Table 8-12; requires Run Franchise
- **Little Italy:** See Table 8-13; requires Grow Population
- **Picnic Tables:** See Table 8-14; requires Central Park
- **Restaurant Research:** See Table 8-15; requires State Fair Pitch
- **Supply Capital City:** See Table 8-16; requires New Fire Station
- **The Date Is On:** See Table 8-17; requires Dress for Date

Table 8-3	Farmin' with Rita	
Quest	*Tasks*	*Reward*
Farmin' with Rita	Harvest four crops Plant four crops	Gray Bunny
The Lost Bunny	Place the Gray Bunny	50 Coins
Rita's Rent	Collect rent from Rita's Country Home	25 Goods

Table 8-4	The Pastry Tour	
Quest	*Tasks*	*Reward*
The Pastry Tour	Click one neighbor's business Click one neighbor's house	25 Goods
The Fussy Baker	Ask two friends to send chocolate (or spend 2 City Cash to skip)	1 Energy

Table 8-5	Find Hidden Key	
Quest	*Tasks*	*Reward*
Find Hidden Key	Harvest four carrots	100 Coins and Family Album
Clear Neighbor's Trees	Clear five trees in neighboring cities	50 Goods
Build Paul a Home	Have a Country Home Place five decorations	100 Coins
Family Feast	Harvest four crops	1 Energy

Table 8-6	Scout Train Routes	
Quest	*Tasks*	*Reward*
Scout Train Routes	Visit five neighboring cities (you need five neighbors to complete this quest)	50 Goods
Send Trains	Run the train three times	100 Coins
Get Charlie Breakfast	Have one danish collectible by collecting from Bakeries	1 Energy

Table 8-7	Expand Franchise	
Quest	*Tasks*	*Reward*
Expand Franchise	Expand a franchise to two locations	1 Experience Point
Franchise Expert	Supply your franchises five times Place one empty lot	2 Energy

Table 8-8	Place Picnic Tables	
Quest	*Tasks*	*Reward*
Place Picnic Tables	Place two Picnic Tables Place five Shade Trees	50 Goods
Move Ruth's Picnic Table	Move two Picnic Tables Move two Shade Trees	50 Coins
Harvest Bird Feed	Harvest six corn	**Museum unlocked**
Place Museum	Place the completed museum	1 Energy
Unlock Love Letter	Harvest six crops	1 Energy

Table 8-9	Helpin' Rita	
Quest	*Tasks*	*Reward*
Helpin' Rita	Harvest six strawberries Collect from houses 12 times	2 Experience Points
Crop Help	Harvest five neighbor's crops Water five neighbor's crops	1 Energy

Table 8-10	Build a Playground	
Quest	*Tasks*	*Reward*
Build a Playground	Have a Swing Set Playground Place five decorations	**Stop Sign unlocked**
School Safety	Place two Stop Signs Place five sidewalks	100 Coins

Table 8-11   Captain's Trip

Quest	Tasks	Reward
Captain's Trip	Unload two Shanghai shippings Unload two Sydney sails	200 Coins
To the Americas!	Unload four New York novelties Unload four Rio routes Unload four San Francisco supplies	1 Energy
Sail the Far Atlantic	Unload four London liners Unload four Paris parcels Unload four Rome relics	2 Energy
Deliver the Goods	Send ten trains	**Red Lighthouse Unlocked**

Table 8-12   Cinema Investment

Quest	Tasks	Reward
Cinema Investment	Have 120,000 Coins	10 Energy
Build Cinema	Have a Cinema Expand Franchise to 5 Locations	3 Experience Points
Cinema Tour	Send 20 Tour Buses	2 Energy

Table 8-13   Little Italy

Quest	Tasks	Reward
Little Italy	Have four Brownstones Place six decorations	200 Coins
Italian Restaurant	Collect rent from Brownstone 20 times	2 Energy
Build Restaurant	Have an Italian Restaurant	100 Goods

Table 8-14   Picnic Tables

Quest	Tasks	Reward
Picnic Tables	Place three Picnic Tables	**Park Plaza unlocked**
Park Beautification	Have a Park Plaza decoration Visit ten neighbors	2 Experience Points

Table 8-15	Restaurant Research	
Quest	**Tasks**	**Reward**
Restaurant Research	Send ten Tour Buses Supply your franchise ten times	100 Goods
Restaurant Food	Collect one carrot soup collectible by harvesting carrots Collect one pie collectible by collecting from Coffee Shops Collect one coffee collectible by collecting from Coffee Shops	**French Restaurant unlocked**
Build Restaurant	Have a French Restaurant	100 Goods

Table 8-16	Supply Capital City	
Quest	**Tasks**	**Reward**
Supply Capital City	Harvest ten cranberries Harvest ten wheat	200 Coins
Crop Tending	Water 15 neighbor crops Revive 15 neighbor crops Harvest 15 neighbor crops	1 Energy
Harvest Peas	Harvest 20 peas	200 Coins
Build Corner Store	Have a Corner Store Collect from the Corner Store Harvest 20 crops	2 Experience Points

Table 8-17	The Date Is On	
Quest	**Tasks**	**Reward**
The Date Is On	Collect from the Sushi Bar five times Collect from the Cinema five times Have two popcorn collectibles by collecting from Cinemas	2 Experience Points
Doc's Date Plan	Have a French Restaurant Have three orchid collectibles by collecting from Flower Kiosks Collect from the French Restaurant three times	2 Energy

Quest	Tasks	Reward
Date Tripping	Collect five Rio routes	200 Coins
Date on Track	Send ten trains	100 Goods
Even More L'Amour	Collect five Paris parcels	2 Energy

Building an Efficient City

A city is more than the buildings and decorations that make it up. The precise arrangement and use of those buildings and decorations can be the difference between a city that works like a well-oiled machine, and one that's stuck like a set of gummed up gears.

This chapter is full of placement and usage tips to really get your city humming. We tell you which types of buildings are most important, how to use your precious Energy, and even the order you should perform common city tasks.

Maximizing Your Land Use

When you start your city in CityVille, you notice a lot of empty space just waiting to be filled with development. Some players simply throw up a random assortment of buildings, decorations, and crops, hoping the result will evolve into a functional city somehow. Putting some thought and care into the placement and balance of your city, on the other hand, can help ensure that your city is the model of efficiency.

Here's how to make sure your limited land is being put to the best possible use.

Choose sidewalks over roads

If there's one bit of land advice every CityVille newcomer needs to know, it's to choose sidewalks over roads. Although every business and housing unit needs to be *connected* to a road to be useful, these buildings don't need to be directly *adjacent* to a road. The key to the distinction is the sidewalk, a 20-Coin decoration that acts as a walkway for your citizens to get to and from their houses and businesses. As long as your sidewalk forms a connected path to a piece of road at one end, all the buildings along that sidewalk count as *connected* and are, therefore, usable.

At first glance, the sidewalk might seem much less economical than its asphalt alternative. After all, a 10-Coin piece of road offers three blocks worth of usable space on each side, whereas it would cost 60 Coins to get that same useful space alongside three separate sidewalk decorations. But the road actually comes with a hidden cost — its three-block thickness. Compared to the thinner sidewalk, the equivalent piece of road takes up six extra blocks of city space that could be used for better purposes. This may not seem like such a big deal, but trust us, those extra blocks of space start to add up as your city expands outward from its small hamlet beginnings.

The only reason to keep more than a single, solitary square of asphalt road is for aesthetic purposes — some city managers like the suburban sprawl look of the blacktop. Other than that, though, feel free to plow away all but one square of asphalt road and replace it with some much more efficient sidewalks.

Don't waste your sidewalk space

Every square of sidewalk space is a square that could be better used for something else. Therefore, you want to have the absolute bare minimum of sidewalks in your town.

Primarily, this means making sure that every square inch of space adjacent to a sidewalk could be used for a house or business. Things like farmland, Goods storage buildings, community buildings, franchise headquarters, and piers don't need to be connected to sidewalks, and therefore should be packed together as tightly as possible in any disused corner of your available city space. Decorations should likewise be placed behind or between buildings, and not next to sidewalks (see the "Placing Decorations Effectively" section, later in the chapter).

Each sidewalk can support two rows of buildings — one on each side. This means that two rows of buildings can be packed right next to each other, if needed, as long as each one has a sidewalk on the other side. Figure 9-1 shows an example of inefficient sidewalk use in which there are two rows of sidewalk connected to a single row of Family Townhomes.

Figure 9-1: The sidewalk row near the top of this figure is redundant.

Denser is better

When building housing in your city, there are a lot of competing variables you might want to consider; however, the only question you really need to pay attention to is this: How much population do you get per square of city space?

In a strictly utilitarian sense, housing in CityVille is simply a means to an end, and that end is more population. Your goal, when building houses, is to achieve that end while using up as little of your limited city space as possible.

After you have a few high-value businesses in town, you'll barely even consider collecting those paltry rents from your houses. So why take those rents into account when purchasing the house? The amount of money you spend on the house is also largely immaterial — after all, you're placing that house for the long haul, and you'll be making that money back in spades soon. Density is really all that matters.

The one exception to the "denser is better" rule may be the Country Home. Early in the game, when you have few resources and even fewer buildings, the ability to collect free Experience Points from a Country Home every five minutes may be worth the sacrifice in density. After you have some high-end businesses and farmland to take up your Energy, however, trade in that Country Home for something a little denser.

Table 9-1 lays out the population density of each housing building in the game. When choosing which house to build, simply choose the building with the highest density that's both available and affordable. (Consult Chapter 4 for unlocking requirements, costs, and other statistics for these buildings.)

Table 9-1	Population Density of Various Housing Options		
Name	**Population**	**Size**	**Density**
Penthouse Tower	220	3 x 3	24.44
Parkside Villa*	350	4 x 4	21.88
Midtown Apartments	310	4 x 4	19.38
Bay Point Duplex	230	4 x 4	14.38
Colonial Chalet	120	3 x 3	13.33
TV Terrace	190	4 x 4	11.88
Newlywed House	100	3 x 3	11.11
Lake House**	90	3 x 3	10.00
Glass Condos	160	4 x 4	10.00
Skyscraper Condos	150	4 x 4	9.38
Stylish Contemporary	80	3 x 3	8.89
Spring Bungalow	72	3 x 3	8.00
Terraced Brownstone	70	3 x 3	7.78
Sprawling Mansion	140	3 x 6	7.78
Hotel Suites	130	3 x 6	7.22
Upscale Condos	110	4 x 4	6.88
Atrium Lofts	170	5 x 5	6.80
Ranch House	100	4 x 4	6.25
Courtyard House**	150	5 x 5	6.00
Apartment Complex	90	4 x 4	5.63
Modern Chateau	60	4 x 4	3.75
Loft Apartments	50	4 x 4	3.13
Suburban House	40	4 x 4	2.50
Country Home	30	4 x 4	1.88
Family Townhouse	20	4 x 4	1.25
Cozy Cottage	10	3 x 3	1.11

The Paradise Villa can't be purchased; it can only be won through the daily raffle.
**These buildings cost City Cash rather than City Coins.*

The road to happiness

Your CityVille population isn't just a number — it's also an emotion. Look in the bottom-left corner of the CityVille play area, just above your neighbor bar, and you see a little Face icon next to your city name and population count. This face represents the general happiness of your citizens:

- A green smiling face means your citizens are happy.
- A yellow grinning face means they're unhappy.
- A morose blue face means they're very sad.

Your citizens' happiness is completely a function of the ratio of the population to the population limit in your town. If your total population is less than 75 percent of the population limit, everyone's perfectly *happy*. A population from 76 to 89 percent of the population limit means *unhappy* citizens, whereas using 90 percent or more of your population cap leads to *sad* citizens. That's right; your town can have 10,000 people and a single restaurant, but as long as you have enough community buildings pumping up that population limit, your citizens will be blissful. Go figure.

Although seeing a sad face representing your citizens is a bit depressing, we haven't been able to figure out any actual, tangible drawback to keeping the citizenry permanently depressed. As far as we can tell, sad citizens are just as content to while away their meaningless virtual lives in a never-ending cycle of consumerism just as efficiently as their more chipper counterparts.

The main function of your population's happiness, as far as we can tell, is a shorthand way to let you know that you're going to have to build some more community buildings before your next house. Personally, we think it's a bit extreme for that basic purpose, but we do have to admit, it is effective at grabbing the player's attention.

As the game continues, you'll likely unlock and be able to afford even denser buildings. When this happens, don't be afraid to destroy your existing housing and replace it with more efficient buildings. You also want your community buildings to provide the most population potential with a minimum city footprint. In general, more expensive community buildings that allow for more people provide a better bang-for-the-space, as it were. There are some exceptions, however, as shown in Table 9-2. Again, in general it's worth investing more money in a more expensive community building that will provide better efficiency rather than scrimping on one that will take up more space for the same value.

The Carousel is an especially small and useful community building that's available earlier and more cheaply than some other highly efficient community buildings.

Table 9-2	Community Building Efficiency		
Name	**Population Allowance**	**Size**	**Efficiency (Population Increase Per Square of City Space)**
Observatory	1,900	4 x 4	118.75
Court House	1,700	4 x 4	106.25
Carousel	700	3 x 3	77.77
Modern Art Gallery	1,900	5 x 5	76
Middle School	800	4 x 4	50
Firehouse	900	6 x 3	50
Baseball Field	1,500	6 x 6	41.66
Mint*	1,000	6 x 4	41.66
Hospital	1,300	8 x 4	40.63
Capitol Building*	1,000	5 x 5	40
Grade School	500	4 x 4	31.25
High School	1,100	6 x 6	30.56
Zynga Gazette	450	4 x 4	28.13
Library	400	4 x 4	25
Television Tower	350	4 x 4	21.88
Museum	300	4 x 4	18.75
Bank	250	4 x 4	15.63
Visitor's Center*	230	4 x 4	14.38
Emergency Clinic	200	4 x 4	12.5
Police	100	3 x 3	11.11
Wedding Hall	70	3 x 3	7.78
City Hall	50	4 x 4	3.13
Post Office	50	4 x 4	3.13

* These community buildings can't be purchased with Coins, only received as rewards.

Businesses über alles

As the most efficient money makers in the game, businesses are truly the engine that drives most CityVille cities. You can think of everything else in the game as being subservient to this engine — the farmland provides the Goods needed for businesses, the houses provide population that frequents the businesses, the decorations provide bonuses to make the businesses more efficient, and so on. Granted, this is a depressingly utilitarian and capitalistic view of the city, but if you want to max out that Coin count, it's the only view of the city that makes sense.

Here are the three main ways of looking at a business, from an economic point of view:

- **How long it will take to pay for itself:** How many times you will need to collect rent from that business before it becomes purely profitable, after your initial investment

- **How efficient it is:** How much money it generates for each precious good put into it

- **How many actual Coins it produces each time you collect rent:** This is the "base" payout for that business

All these numbers are important, but in general, businesses with better Goods-to-earnings ratios and base payouts are better than less efficient business that pay for themselves more quickly. To understand why this is, think about the long term. For example, compare Mayor A, who spends 100,000 to establish a Cinema, with Mayor B, who spends just 35,000 Coins on a Shoe Store.

After five collections for each city, Mayor B has paid for his investment, whereas Mayor A is still almost 95,000 Coins in the hole. But look at things in a little longer term: In the future, both mayors have invested 500,000 Goods into their respective businesses and collected earnings from them thousands of times. At this point, Mayor A has made nearly 2.5 million Coins in profit from his Cinema, whereas Mayor B has made a bit less than 2.2 million Coins — quite the difference.

Pumping 500,000 Goods into your business a few hundred at a time takes awhile. But CityVille is designed to be a game you play day in, day out with no set end point.

The long-term profitability equation looks even better if your businesses are enhanced by some profit-boosting decorations. Higher-base earnings are the name of the game here — after all, a 20-percent bonus on 900 Coins is a lot better than a 20-percent bonus on 600 Coins. See Chapter 12, where we discuss using Tower Eats for more on the benefits of high-base earnings.

Although you may need to buy some self-sustaining businesses early on, as your money situation becomes more stable, focus on the highly efficient businesses that will convert your Goods into the most Coins well into the future.

Table 9-3 shows which businesses provide the most Coins for each good you put in and which ones pay for themselves most quickly. We left out businesses you can buy only with City Cash, as well as businesses you can earn only through other means outside of the Build menu.

Table 9-3	Business Efficiency				
Business	*Cost (Coins)*	*Earnings (Coins)*	*Supply (Goods)*	*Coins Per Good*	*Collections to Profit*
Sushi Bar	12,500	605	110	5.5	21
Handbag Store	10,000	654	120	5.45	16
Tower Eats	1,000,000	900	165	5.45	1,112
Music Store	900,000	881	163	5.4	1,022
Wedding Store	15,000	702	130	5.4	22
Furniture Store	750,000	864	160	5.4	869
Cinema	100,000	749	140	5.35	134
Jewelry Store	500,000	830	155	5.35	603
Chic Boutique	250,000	795	150	5.3	315
Video Game Store	1,300	50	10	5	26
Cosmetic Store	1,900	120	25	4.8	16
Diner	1,600	230	50	4.6	7
Noodle Shop	4,000	405	90	4.5	10
City Dojo	4,250	495	11	4.5	9
French Restaurant	4,500	495	110	4.5	10
Laundromat	5,000	515	115	4.48	10
Sunglasses Store	5,500	534	120	4.45	11
Tofu Burger	5,000	507	115	4.41	10
Bike Shop	2,500	330	75	4.4	8
Shoe Store	3,500	572	130	4.4	7
City Supermarket	5,750	569	130	4.38	11
Department Store	8,000	588	135	4.35	14
Seafood Restaurant	7,500	609	140	4.35	13
Bookstore	3,000	430	100	4.3	7
Packing Store	3,000	430	100	4.3	7

Business	Cost (Coins)	Earnings (Coins)	Supply (Goods)	Coins Per Good	Collections to Profit
Italian Restaurant	6,500	645	150	4.3	11
Pool Hall	2,200	420	100	4.2	6
Bakery	200	40	10	4	5
Flower Kiosk	400	95	25	3.8	5
Toy Store	800	180	50	3.6	5
Coffee Shop	600	320	100	3.2	2
Burger Joint	1,000	240	75	3.2	5

You can never farm too much

At first glance, farmland might seem like a waste of precious space. After all, farmland takes in money without directly giving any back, but it's valuable because the Goods it provides help drive the profit engine that is your city's businesses. In fact, with a good, decorated business to feed into, crop space can be one of the most efficient uses of your land.

With that in mind, how much farmland (and storage space) do you actually need to purchase? At first, the answer seems like it should be "as much as you can afford." For instance, more farmland means you can harvest more crops in the same amount of time. More harvested crops means more Goods, and more Goods means more money from your businesses.

You have a few limits on the amount of farmland you need, though. For one, if you have too many plots of farmland, you may not have the Energy to harvest all your crops or the storage to store the excess after all your businesses are supplied. If you constantly have trouble harvesting and storing your crops before they wither and die, even though you prioritize your harvests, remove a few squares or farmland and replace them with storage buildings, such as Sticks. This strategy helps you keep a good balance between Goods storage and crop space.

Excessive farmland can also get in the way of the natural expansion of your city. If you struggle to find new space to put news sidewalks and businesses while never lacking in Goods to supply the businesses you already have, it may be time to cut back on the farmland.

Avoid gaps

This final bit of land advice appeals to the more geometrically inclined players. As you've probably noticed, every item in CityVille has a rectangular footprint marking the space it takes up, which appears as a green grid when you place or move an item on the map.

This rectangular regularity means you can easily position all your various buildings and decorations packed tightly next to one another, with no gaps in between. This is important because gaps are wasted space. Remember, you can use the Move tool and the Rotate tool to rearrange your items until they fit together nicely.

Figure 9-2 shows a set of community buildings arranged tightly, without any gaps. Figure 9-3 shows a set of buildings arranged sloppily, with plenty of gaps, and more space taken up by the same buildings from Figure 9-2. Notice how much less total space the arrangement in Figure 9-2 uses, allowing for further development right next to the grouping.

Figure 9-2: A tight arrangement of community buildings.

Figure 9-3: A looser arrangement of the same buildings.

Managing Your Energy Effectively

After city space, Energy is the most limited resource in the game. True, you can always get more Energy simply by waiting awhile for your Energy meter to slowly fill up. But who wants to do that? You have a city to run and you want to run it now, not later!

Unfortunately, the only 100-percent guaranteed way to get more Energy immediately requires spending Cash on Energy Batteries in the Build menu, as we discuss in Chapter 4. Fortunately, you can do a couple of things to make sure you maximize the Energy available to you and get the most return for each Energy you spend.

Maximizing your available Energy

With Energy being such an important commodity, making sure you get and use as much of it as possible is the key to efficiently maintaining your city. The following sections offer some tips for maximizing the amount of Energy available to you throughout your time in CityVille.

Check CityVille as soon as your Energy meter is filled

As we discuss in Chapter 7, you automatically get one more unit of Energy every five minutes, even if you're not actively playing the game during that time. There's only one exception to this otherwise inviolable rule — when your Energy meter is already full, you can't automatically gain any more Energy.

For this reason, check in to CityVille as soon as possible after your Energy meter fills up. Calculating the timing of this couldn't be simpler. First, be sure to note your maximum Energy level before you get started on your CityVille session. Then, when you've done everything you can in your city for the day and depleted your Energy meter completely, note the current time. Add five minutes for each Energy your meter can hold and then mark down the time when you need to return to use some more Energy. Set an alarm or a countdown timer if you think it'll help.

After you reach Level 28, you're capped at a maximum of 30 Energy in your meter. That means you have 150 minutes — or two and a half hours — between the time your Energy is depleted and the time it's completely full again. This standard time allows you to get into a good rhythm throughout the day, taking a quick *Energy break* every two to three hours just to make sure you're doing the most you can in your city.

Of course, you can check on your city before your Energy meter is completely full to skim off a few quick clicks. In fact, this is often a good time-management strategy if you know you're going to be busy when your Energy meter would fill up.

Say you have a business meeting from 1 p.m. to 3 p.m., for instance, and your Energy meter is set to be full again at 1:30. You could just skip that check-in, essentially throwing away the Energy-earning time between 1:30 and 3 p.m. Alternatively, you could visit your city just before your meeting. You'd get to use the mostly-full Energy meter you've accumulated at 12:45 p.m. or so, and then come back after your meeting to a meter that's nearly full again! Now that's smart Energy management!

If you don't have any conflicting appointments, though, we recommend waiting until your Energy meter is completely full before coming back to your city. Not only do more frequent check-ins quickly get annoyingly cumbersome but a full Energy meter also maximizes your opportunity to use the Bonus bar for extra Coins (see Chapter 14 for more on the Bonus bar).

The Energy meter limit applies only to Energy earned automatically by waiting. Energy gained by using Batteries, visiting neighbors, and collecting from community buildings can actually *overfill* your Energy meter, temporarily extending your maximum Energy. Such an overfilled Energy meter has the total available Energy displayed as a green number, as shown in Figure 9-4. This Energy stays in the meter until it's used, but remember, an overfilled meter has to be depleted that much more before the passage of time starts automatically filling it again.

Figure 9-4: An overfilled Energy meter.

Visit and help your neighbors as often as possible

Sure, free Goods, Coins, and Experience Points are decent perks for visiting and helping your neighbors' cities. But these perks pale in comparison to the wonder that is free Energy points. If correctly managed, this extra Energy can be like a free, extra full Energy meter every day — one you don't have to wait a full 150 minutes to get!

Because you get your free Energy as soon as you visit a neighbor, it might be tempting to just pop in and then pop right back home to use your new-gotten abilities. Resist that urge, though, and spend a few seconds clicking around to help your neighbor's city. Remember, the amount of free Energy you can get daily from your neighbors is limited by your Reputation level, and the only way to raise that is to collect the Heart icons that spill out when you actively help in a neighbor's city.

The time you spend helping your neighbors is also time your Energy meter naturally refills (assuming it's not full). So take your time helping, safe in the knowledge that you'll have more Energy when you return.

Don't forget your community buildings

If you're focused on harvesting crops and collecting earnings from businesses, it can be easy to forget to collect from those community buildings sitting harmlessly in the corner of your city. This would be a mistake, though. Although you may think collecting from these businesses seems like a waste of Energy, collecting from community buildings is actually often a great way to produce more Energy than you're putting in.

As shown in Table 9-4, most community buildings come with a relatively high chance of producing at least 1 Energy when you make your daily collection. In fact, eight community buildings always produce at least 1 Energy per collection, effectively making them free, once-daily Coin machines. For some of these community buildings, in fact, there's a better-than-even chance that your collection produces 2 or more replacement Energy, effectively making them once-daily Energy creation machines! What a deal!

Table 9-4	Getting Energy Rewards from Community Buildings		
Name	**Chance of Getting at Least 1 Energy (%)**	**Change of Getting at Least 2 Energy (%)**	**Chance of Getting at Least 3 Energy (%)**
Baseball Field	100	60	20
Court House	100	60	10
Modern Art Gallery	100	60	10
Hospital	100	60	10
Observatory	100	50	10
High School	100	50	10
Carousel	100	50	0
Middle School	100	50	0
Mint*	90	50	0
Firehouse	90	50	0
Capitol Building*	90	50	0
Grade School	90	40	0
Museum	90	40	0

(continued)

Table 9-4 *(continued)*

Name	Chance of Getting at Least 1 Energy (%)	Change of Getting at Least 2 Energy (%)	Chance of Getting at Least 3 Energy (%)
Zynga Gazette	70	40	0
Library	70	40	0
Bank	70	30	0
Emergency Clinic	70	30	0
Police	60	30	0
Wedding Hall	50	30	0
Post Office	50	30	0
City Hall	50	20	0

* Community buildings that can't be bought with Coins.

Send Energy to your neighbors

You know how sometimes devoting your Energy to helping someone else can, paradoxically, help you feel more energized and full of life in the real world? The same thing can happen virtually in CityVille. When you send Energy Batteries to your neighbors in the game (see Chapter 6), it's more than likely that some of those neighbors will take the opportunity to click the Send One Back button and return the favor by giving you an Energy Battery of your very own. Remember, you can just as easily send one back again, continuing the cycle of Energy sharing and camaraderie that is at the heart of social gaming.

Using your Energy wisely

If you've followed the steps in the earlier sections of this chapter, you're swimming in as much Energy as you can possibly tolerate. Now's the time to make sure you know what to do with all that Energy. Not every click is created equal, after all, and wasting your Energy on anything less than its very best use is like throwing your Energy down the, uh, electrical socket.

When in doubt, harvest first

When you first visit a bustling city, it can be hard to know which shiny icon to click first. In general, harvesting as many ripe crops as possible to start a session is never a bad idea, assuming you have some excess storage capacity for those Goods.

Although ripened crops can wither and die on their plots, the Goods they provide never spoil when stored in a storage building. Therefore, extracting the Goods from those fragile crops is a time-sensitive affair. Those Goods can then be converted into a lot of Coins through your businesses, so it's almost never a bad idea to fill those storage buildings when you can (or to build more storage buildings, if you have the room and the money).

Don't forget about any ships you might have sent out for Goods-producing shipping missions as well (see Chapter 7). You might overlook this area of your city as you focus on your farm, but keep in mind that the Goods on deck can spoil just as easily as the crops in your field.

Some businesses are better than others

Using Energy to collect earnings from businesses is almost never a bad idea. But collecting from some businesses rather than from others can be a better idea.

As most cities grow, they start to accumulate a wide variety of businesses in their limits, with all sorts of different returns on the Goods and Energy you invest in them. Obviously, you shouldn't waste Energy collecting from that rinky-dink Bakery if there's a fully decorated Cinema just waiting to give up its lucrative gold bars.

But after you collect from the Cinema, ask whether that rinky-dink Bakery is *ever* worth collecting from. Sure, the Bakery was worthwhile early in the game when it was all you could afford, but now that you have better businesses around, the Energy you use collecting a few hundred Coins from that tiny Bakery could probably be better used elsewhere, or even saved to collect from a high-earning business sooner.

In general, if you're constantly disappointed by the small Coin icons coming out of a business or are sighing audibly when you use your Energy on a business, consider tearing down that building and investing in something a bit more productive. The expense hurts in the short run, but trust us, you'll feel better in the long run.

Don't waste your Energy collecting rent from housing. After you've been playing CityVille for a while, chances are you have a good number of housing units sitting around, and chances are a little Coin icon hovers over them all begging you to spend Energy clicking them to collect the rent that's due to you as the Mayor.

We know it's tempting. We know it seems like a no-brainer. But listen to us when we say: Do not waste your Energy collecting rent from housing.

Why shouldn't you accept the game's essentially free gift of rent money? Why is it a good idea to ignore all those hovering Coins? The answer is simple — although the Coins from housing rent are nice, there's almost definitely something better you could be doing with that Energy. And if there isn't, there should be.

All but the smallest, most inefficient businesses produce more Coins per click than even the most lucrative of houses. It's just that simple. Yes, you probably used a little bit more Energy to harvest the Goods that went into the businesses earnings, but if you're planting efficient crops, such as peas, and using train and shipping missions wisely (see Chapter 7), this shouldn't be a big issue. By the time you're buying big businesses, such as Sushi Bars and Cinemas (see Chapter 12), and decorating them effectively, it's not even a contest anymore — businesses blow housing out of the water for their earnings-per-Energy potential.

The only exception to this general rule comes very early in the game, when you may want to collect rent from Country Homes on a quick, five-minute cycle to quickly increase your Experience Points and level. Don't let this exception become the rule though; break the habit by Level 10 at the very latest. Even if none of your businesses is ready to produce earnings, that's still no reason to throw good remaining Energy after collecting housing rent. You could spend that Energy harvesting crops, after all — crops that will go into future business earnings. Or, if you don't have any ripe crops, you could put the Energy into chopping down trees or developing new buildings for your recently purchased expansions. Or, if you don't have any land to use, you could just sit on that Energy and return to a full Energy bar that much sooner.

Don't waste Energy just because you can

Just because you have Energy left over doesn't mean you should waste it on tasks that are less than lucrative. That same Energy you're spending collecting rent from a low-earning house could go toward collecting from a business. That same Energy that you're wasting on that low-earning business could instead go toward harvesting crops for a better business.

If you're constantly finding yourself with too much Energy and not enough worthwhile to do with it, you probably need to invest in some more businesses, farmland, or storage space. If you don't have enough space to place those things, work on getting another land expansion going for your city. In any case, the Energy you'd be throwing away could be put toward setting up worthwhile new buildings.

Use train missions

Why spend Energy when you don't have to? What a silly question. If you can get an in-game benefit without using your precious Energy, you'd take it, right? Well, that's the opportunity provided all the time by train missions.

As we detail in Chapter 7, train missions take money and return it minutes or hours later in the form of Goods. There are plenty of downsides to train missions, though. For one, they cost a lot of money for the amount of Goods you get back, at least when compared with most crops. For another, you can have only one train mission out at a time, which can be especially annoying and inefficient if you send for one of the multi-day missions.

But there's one crucial benefit to the train mission — it's one of the only ways of getting in-game Goods without spending any Energy. Especially focus on the CharlieVille train mission, (assuming you've unlocked it by completing the appropriate goal; see Chapter 8). Sure, this mission costs a whole lot of Coins for a relatively paltry return of 300 Goods, but those Goods come back in five minutes and don't cost you a single, precious Energy point. Cha-ching!

Maximize your Bonus bar

When you're in the grip of a budding CityVille addiction, it might be tempting to sit anxiously by an open CityVille window, watching that Next Energy In timer count down and waiting with an itchy finger to click a deserving crop or business at the very first possible moment.

This would be a decent — if life-consuming — idea, except for one factor: the Bonus bar. As we discuss in Chapter 14, the Bonus bar provides extra Coins when you spend a lot of Energy in a quick sequence. So if you're waiting impatiently by the screen, using 1 Energy every five minutes, you're essentially giving up thousands of bonus Coins that you could get by saving that Energy for one big burst of activity.

Of course, saving up for too long is also not good — remember, your Energy meter can fill up only until it's full; after that, any time spent away from the game is essentially wasted Energy. On the whole, though, it's probably better to give up a little bit of Energy by checking in late than to give up a lot of Coins by never leaving the game. This is true even if you don't consider the harm to your work and social life caused by never leaving your computer.

Perform common city tasks in an efficient order

Getting the most out of your city isn't just a matter of obtaining and using Energy efficiently. The order in which you perform many common city tasks can affect the returns you get from those tasks, as we outline in this section. Furthermore, having a checklist of regular tasks to perform every time you visit your city can be handy to make sure you don't forget anything crucial.

Don't be afraid to intersperse some quick, five-minute train missions to CharlieVille at odd points in between steps, when you find a moment. The quick, Energy-efficient Goods provided by these visits can help with supply issues.

Here's the order of tasks you need perform every time you visit your city:

1. **Check your Facebook News Feed for bonus opportunities.**

   As we outline in Chapter 6, your News Feed can be an underappreciated source of bonus Goods, Coins, and Experience Points that can be obtained with just a click. Before you actually load up your CityVille game, do a quick scan and see whether any new bonuses have been posted.

2. **Accept any gifts from neighbors and give gifts to neighbors.**

   It's pretty hard to forget to accept gifts sent to you because the CityVille Messages tab appears first thing every time you load CityVille. But it's a lot easier to forget to send gifts to your neighbors. Remember this crucial step, though, because sending gifts to neighbors is the best way to encourage them to send gifts back. Obviously, if you've reached your in-game gift-giving limit for the day, you can skip this step.

3. **Visit and help your neighbors.**

   It may seem silly to put your neighbors before yourself, but the bonus Energy you get for visiting and helping comes in handy later when you're racking up those bonuses. Of course, if you've already helped as many neighbors as you can for the day, don't bother visiting just to say hi. Also, if your Goods storage is already full to the brim, you may want to postpone your visits until a little later. Some players also prefer to visit their neighbors when their Energy meter is already depleted, allowing it to refill as they work in other metropolises. Your mileage may vary.

4. **Supply as many unsupplied businesses as possible.**

   Those businesses with that little Box icon over them are businesses that aren't busy producing the Coins you want. You probably supplied as many businesses as possible when you finished your last city visit, of course, but the new Goods you got from your Facebook News Feed, neighbor visits, or early train missions can be pumped into those unproductive businesses immediately.

5. **Use any Energy Batteries you received as gifts.**

   In addition to the Energy you may have gotten from visiting neighbors, these batteries help you overfill your Energy meter, giving you the maximum possible ability to rack up bonuses in Steps 6–8.

6. **Accept help from neighbors.**

   If there are any hovering Neighbor avatars sitting over your city, this is the time to click them to receive the free work they provide for your city (see Chapter 6 for more on accepting help in your city from your neighbors). By accepting this help before spending your Energy, you're making sure your efforts and those of your neighbors don't overlap and that your Energy will go to its best possible uses. The only reason to hesitate here is if your Goods storage is already full and your neighbors have helped you with harvesting.

Your helpful neighbors drop Resource icons as they assist around your city. Be ready to click those icons and keep your Bonus bar going as you track their progress. Don't hesitate to move on to the next step and keep the Bonus bar going as you start to spend your Energy.

7. **If possible, collect from all community buildings.**

These buildings provide a whopping 5 Coins and 1 Energy (and sometimes up to 3 Energy) when clicked, which can all be vacuumed up by your hungry mouse to send that Bonus bar into the stratosphere. Plus, the extra Energy is likely to keep your Energy meter overfilled as you move on to Step 8.

8. **Harvest crops/ships, collect from businesses, and supply those businesses.**

These three actions are grouped together because they're all performed together, in an improvisational cycle that has to adjust along with conditions. The goal here is to keep your Bonus bar going for as long as possible, while simultaneously keeping your Goods storage level from getting too full or too low. If your Goods level is too low, harvest some crops, making sure to click the Resource icons quickly to continue the bonus. As your Goods fill up, start collecting from businesses and resupplying them to give yourself room to harvest again. Be careful, though — resupplying businesses takes time and doesn't provide any Bonus bar–maintaining Resource icons, so make sure some are lying around for you to collect.

If you've managed things correctly, you can deplete your entire Energy reserves in this step without once letting the Bonus bar restart, all the while racking up tons of Coins and Goods. If you run out of ripe crops or ready businesses, however, move on to Step 9.

9. **If possible, work on expansion.**

If you have more Energy than you know what to do with, now's the perfect time to plow some of it to improve your city by erecting buildings. Don't have room for any more buildings? Look into an expansion. Don't have the building permits for an expansion? Time to bug your neighbors!

10. **Replant your crops.**

Now that you're out of Energy, do the cleanup tasks that don't require Energy expenditures. This includes replanting the fields of crops that you just harvested. Forgetting this step is a good way to find yourself without the necessary Goods to supply your businesses later, so be sure to make it a priority.

11. **If you have franchises, supply them.**

    Another task that's easy to overlook is supplying your franchises (and collecting the daily bonus from your headquarters). This is a good way to make some extra Coins. See Chapter 6 for more on this.

12. **Supply any businesses that need it.**

    If you have any leftover Goods and any businesses that are in need of supplying, now's the perfect time to supply them. This way they'll be ready to give up those precious Coins when your Energy is refilled and you're ready for another round.

Placing Decorations Effectively

Any real city slicker knows that a city is more than just the buildings that make it up, or even the people that live in it. Little touches, such as trees, parks and animals, can help a city come to life in all sorts of ways. The same is true in CityVille, where decorations are good for giving your city some aesthetic oomph and for providing some lucrative bonuses to the regular production of housing and businesses.

This chapter discusses both of these uses for using decorations, providing some useful strategies for using them to generate profits and beauty.

Planning decorations for profit

When you place most decorations, you notice a square blue halo on the ground surrounding the position you're about to choose for that decoration. If that blue square intersects with any houses or businesses, you see a set of bonus numbers appear on those buildings, as shown in Figure 9-5. The first number is the percentage bonus provided by the decoration you're placing, and the number in parentheses is the total percentage bonus that building receives when you place the decoration there. That is, every time you collect rent or earnings from that building, you receive that much more money than that building's base value (for more on base values for various buildings, see Chapter 4).

Getting those bonus numbers as high as possible while spending as little money as possible is key to maximizing your CityVille profits. There are two effective methods for getting the most bang for your buck when it comes to decorations, and we outline in the following sections.

Figure 9-5: The decoration bonus on a business, as shown when placing a decoration.

You may notice that we primarily use Rocky Hill and Expo Tent decorations in the examples for both decorating methods. There's a good reason for this — they're among the best decorations in the game, providing larger bonuses than most other decorations that would take up the same space. What's more, the Expo Tent is thin enough that a decoration on one side can provide its bonus to a business immediately on the other side.

We use businesses in these examples rather than housing units. The reason for this is because businesses generally have higher base values than housing. Therefore, the percentage boost from a decoration is worth more on a business than on housing. It's as simple as that.

The Around the Corner method

The general goal of the Around the Corner decorating method is to make sure your decorations each provide their bonus to as many businesses as possible. As shown in Figure 9-6, this means surrounding your decorations with businesses that are usually connected to a corner of your city's sidewalk, thus wrapping the decoration in a protective shell of productive businesses.

Because the Expo Tent is only two blocks thick, the Rocky Hill in the middle of this arrangement manages to impart its 20-percent bonus to all 11 businesses on the periphery. You can even close the sidewalk loop on the other end to get even more businesses in on the act.

Figure 9-6: An example of the Around the Corner decorating method.

The benefit of this method is that it generally maximizes the advantages gained from each expensive decoration you've purchased. Instead of just granting a 20-percent bonus, that Rocky Hill can grant upward of a dozen 20-percent bonuses to various businesses, sending your overall earning potential that much higher without forcing you to buy any more decorations. Even if you don't use this particular configuration, making sure your decoration bonuses touch as many businesses as possible is a good general strategy.

The downside of this strategy is that your distributed bonus is spread across multiple businesses, each of which requires precious Energy and Goods before you can collect its earnings. This might not seems like a big deal early on, when you have only a few buildings, but as your city expands and your Energy meter tops out at 30, it may seem a little more urgent.

The Surround the Business method

The general goal behind the Surround the Business decorating method is to get as many decoration bonuses on a single business as possible. As shown in Figure 9-7, this means surrounding your businesses with a regimented grid of high-value decorations, leaving only a sliver of space for a sidewalk to allow the business to receive customers.

The pattern in the figure here is still incomplete. Each Cinema could be surrounded by a few more Rocky Hills around the inner ring of Expo Tents to truly maximize the stacking bonuses on each. The basic grid pattern started here can be repeated with as many decorations and businesses as you can afford. Also notice that the Rocky Hills in the middle of this arrangement are positioned precisely to give their bonuses to both Cinemas, doubling their effectiveness.

Figure 9-7: The Surround the Business method of decorating.

One more thing: For this method to work as effectively as possible, a business with a big footprint, such as the 4-x-4 Cinema, is necessary. This larger footprint gives more surface area for that decoration halo to reach out and capture a portion for the building to impart its bonus.

With perfect placement, you can get bonuses approaching and exceeding 300 percent on one business. This means that each time you collect earnings from that business, it's like you're collecting from four businesses at once, without spending any more Energy or Goods than normal. Score!

The real downside of this decorating method is that buying so many high-bonus decorations can be extremely expensive, as can the larger businesses that are central to the method. This method is also very space-intensive — a truly regimented grid of decorations in this vein leaves little room for deviation or personal expression. Hey, no one ever said maximizing your profits and being creative would go together.

Placing decorations for fun

For most of this book, we focus on buying and placing items for maximum profitability. But there's more to life than the pursuit of money. What about the pursuit of beauty?

This section has some tips for beautifying your town in some fun and artistic ways.

Creating 3D effects with decorations

One aspect of many cities that's not accurately represented in CityVille is the idea of hills and changing elevations. Luckily, thanks to the games isometric perspective, some clever decoration placement can create the illusion of height in even the flattest of cities.

Figure 9-8 shows a simple example of how a few carefully placed Sturdy Fence decorations, along with a slight shift of nearby businesses, can make a building look like it's on stilts. This is just the tip of the iceberg, though. Players have created the illusions of massive, city-spanning, multi-tiered structures using hundreds of sturdy fences.

Figure 9-8: Whoa, man. That crab shack is floating, but it's still on the ground.

Using decorations as pixel art

Artists who subscribe to the visual style of Pointillism created works in which a series of carefully placed tiny dots created the impression of a much larger, much fuller picture when viewed from afar. The Pointillists would probably love CityVille, which is, after all, just a big grid of dots just waiting to be filled with colorful decorations.

Figure 9-9 shows an incredibly simple example of how this kind of Pointillism can be put to good use in CityVille, by placing flowers in an arrangement that looks like a smiling face. Obviously, from this figure, you can tell that your authors were hired for their writing abilities, not their artistic abilities. But those with a bit more of an artistic bent can extend this idea out, creating truly breathtaking works of art made only of CityVille decorations.

Figure 9-9: Your city is happy to see you.

Part III
Staying Safe and Up to Date on CityVille

The 5th Wave   By Rich Tennant

"Mr. President, North Korean President Kim Jong-il wants to be neighbors in CityVille."

*T*his part of the book focuses on keeping you knowledgeable and safe as you play CityVille online.

Chapter 10 gives you advice on avoiding common CityVille scams and how to contact CityVille's developer Zynga. We also give links to Web resources for you to see what others are saying and how they're playing.

Chapter 11 covers some of the most common technical bugs and glitches and how to work around them.

Staying Secure and Finding Support

*W*ith tens of millions of players, CityVille has attracted a lot of attention from unscrupulous characters looking to exploit some player's lack of technical knowledge through CityVille-related scams. This chapter shows you how to spot some of the most common of these scams so that you can avoid being drawn in.

Despite our best efforts, this book may not be able to answer all your support questions about CityVille. Some issues you encounter may require the help of Zynga support to fix, and we tell you in this chapter how to contact that support. Other issues may have to do with new features introduced after this book goes to press. As a result, in this chapter, we recommend some good Web resources for keeping up with these frequent changes, as well.

Avoiding CityVille Scams

Unfortunately, numerous scams targeted at unsuspecting CityVille players are floating around out there. Most of these scams are designed to make you believe they originate from CityVille, or from its publisher, Zynga, while asking you to reveal private information about you or your account.

Each CityVille player needs to take responsibility to protect his or her personal security while playing the game. Keep an eye out for these common types of scams.

"Free" City Cash offers

Zynga provides links to numerous offers and promotions that purport to provide free in-game City Cash upon completion. Unfortunately, being linked to the CityVille page doesn't mean they're useful or trustworthy.

- ✔ Some offers claim to require only a free trial subscription on the link but then demand an upfront payment after you click through.

- ✔ Others simply refuse to work unless you choose one of the paid options they offer, despite having been advertised as free offers.

- ✔ Still others simply never deliver the City Cash they promise after you complete the offer.

In general, if an offer comes from a major, well-known national brand, it's most likely safe. Be wary of offers from unknown companies that ask you to provide your cellphone number or mailing address. Giving out cellphone numbers in these offers can be especially dangerous because unscrupulous companies can use them to place unwanted charges on your cellphone bill. Always read the fine print on any offer page to make sure you know what you're agreeing to.

If you do run into an offer that you feel is fraudulent in some way, contact Zynga using the methods discussed later in this chapter. After an outcry from many players, the company is pretty good about responding to complaints and cleaning up problems on its Offer page.

It should go without saying that you shouldn't trust any other Web site besides CityVille's that provides links to supposedly free City Cash offers. As a rule, if you didn't find it on the CityVille game page, don't trust it — and even if you did find it on CityVille, be cautious.

CityVille guides

A quick Internet search for CityVille turns up countless guides that promise to make you a better CityVille player by giving you secrets, tips, and strategies that aren't available to the general public.

Of course, you have this book, which does all those things already, so you don't need to search out those guides.

Be cautious of guides that ask for any sort of upfront payment before providing a download. The PDF products they offer are usually no better than the information freely available online (or in a book like the one you're holding!). In extreme cases, the guide itself may not exist, a fact you'll discover only after your credit card has been charged.

You may come across sites that claim if you download so-and-so program, you can bypass game restrictions and gain things like unlimited City Cash and energy. A few words of caution about this method of playing:

- ✔ Zynga, like any software developer, doesn't look kindly upon people playing around with its code to cheat the game. If you're caught doing something like this, you could have your Zynga account shut down and you could be banned from returning to any of its games.

- ✔ Even if these programs *do* work, many contain malicious add-ons like viruses, Trojans, and other nasty things you don't want in your computer. This is another way your personal information could be put at risk. It's just not worth it!

- ✔ Really, doesn't cheating take the fun out of the game?

Fake CityVille Facebook groups

Searching for CityVille-related groups on Facebook easily turns up hundreds and hundreds of groups that claim to offer free City Cash or other items if you become a fan, as shown in Figure 10-1.

These Facebook groups are scams. No exceptions. They use unfulfillable promises of free stuff to attract members.

The only legitimate ways to receive free City Cash are listed in Chapter 7 of the book. Disregard any Facebook groups that say otherwise.

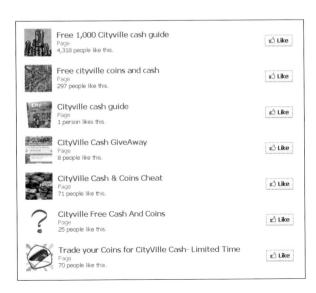

Figure 10-1: Examples of false CityVille promises made by Facebook scam groups.

Protecting Yourself on Facebook

Protecting yourself while playing also means protecting your Facebook account. Zynga will not accept responsibility for any items, City Cash, or City Coins that might be lost if your Facebook account is

- ✓ Accessed illegitimately by a hacker
- ✓ Incorrectly used by someone who has your permission

Allowing other people to access your Facebook account carries serious personal privacy risks. Follow these tips to help protect your Facebook account from illegitimate access:

- ✓ **Never share your Facebook account information with other Facebook users, third-party Web sites, or anyone else.** When you first install the game, Zynga asks permission to access your Facebook account information. This is okay, of course, because you want to play the game! But if a person or a different site says it needs your Facebook information to give you access to a free item or to unlock privileged game features, ignore that request. Your login information should always remain private and known only to you. Type your Facebook password only into the Facebook login page.

- ✓ **Use a strong password.** A strong password includes lowercase and capital letters and numbers and symbols, and it doesn't include words commonly found in a dictionary. Try adapting your password from the first letters of an easy-to-remember phrase or song lyric, or use an easy-to-remember pattern of key positions on your keyboard. Insert memorable dates and numbers into the password for added security. Remember, longer passwords are harder for hackers to figure out.

- ✓ **Use unique login information.** Don't use the same e-mail address and password information for more than one Web site. For simplicity and memorability, try adding some variation of the current site's name to the end of your standard password.

- ✓ **Avoid clicking Facebook News Feed links from unknown parties.** Fake links often try to fool you into entering your Facebook login information so that a third party can record it.

   Be especially careful if Facebook unexpectedly asks you to enter your login information after clicking a link; you may not actually be on Facebook, even if the page looks legitimate. Check the URL in the address bar carefully.

- ✓ **Download a virus scanner and run regular virus scans.** AVG offers a relatively robust, free virus scanner at http://free.avg.com.

- ✔ **Log out after using Facebook on a public computer.** If you don't log out, the next person to use that computer has full access to your Facebook account. Log out by clicking the Account button in the upper-right corner of any Facebook page and then choosing Logout in the drop-down list that appears.

- ✔ **Do not click suspicious third-party CityVille links.** Whenever you see a post on an unofficial CityVille Facebook Page or in a CityVille group saying something like "Get 100 free City Cash now!" chances are it's a phishing scam. Clicking these links takes you to a page outside of Facebook where they will ask you to allow access to your Facebook profile information. Do *not* allow this! These scams are called *phishing,* and they will utilize your Facebook account to post fraudulent messages just like the one you saw. Remember: If an offer seems too good to be true, it probably is.

- ✔ **Beware of e-mails from fake Facebook addresses.** You may receive an e-mail that asks you to, for example, log into your account to verify your information. Be sure to check the address of the person sending this e-mail. Facebook will never send e-mails to its members asking for account information. Many times these e-mail addresses have mis-spelled words in them such as *accounts@fcebook.com*. These e-mails may contain the Facebook logo, but they are fraudulent.

Contacting Zynga

If you run into a technical, billing, or game play issue with CityVille that you can't fix using the information in this book, you can contact the game's publisher, Zynga, for help. The following sections describe ways to seek help from Zynga.

General user support

You can find Zynga's support page by visiting

```
http://support.zynga.com
```

From here, click the CityVille icon in to top menu bar to be taken to the CityVille support page shown in Figure 10-2. Here you can get more information about some of the most common issues currently affecting CityVille players.

More likely, though, you'll want to skip these links and search for the specific information you're looking for:

1. **In the Search box midway down the page on the right side, type a few keywords describing your problem (for example, type** the page freezes when I try to redeem collections**) and then click the Search button.**

   The search results page that appears displays a list of possible answers to your issue.

2. **Click the links on the Results page for information about that issue from Zynga's support database.**

   If your question is answered, you're done!

Figure 10-2: Zynga's CityVille support page.

If you don't find an answer to your issue in your search results, send an e-mail request to Zynga:

1. **Click the See More link on the main support page and then click the Email Us link on the right sidebar.**

   The Zynga e-mail support form, as shown in Figure 10-3, appears.

2. **Use the drop-down lists and text areas to detail the problem you're having and then click the Submit button to send your question to Zynga.**

   The company usually responds to e-mail queries in anywhere from 24 to 48 hours.

Can't wait one to two days to hear back from Zynga? You're in luck because it now has a Chat support option where you can "talk" to a representative right away — or at least after a short wait until a representative becomes free. These chat representatives are extremely helpful, and chatting with them makes it easier to clarify any questions you have because e-mails can sometimes be misunderstood. Plus, if for some reason your question isn't answered via e-mail the first time, you'll have to submit another request via e-mail and start waiting all over again. With a chat, you can clarify any issues then and there. Their chat window is found on the right size of the CityVille help page, as shown in Figure 10-4.

Figure 10-3: Zynga's e-mail support form.

Figure 10-4: Get answers quickly via chat support.

Zynga's support page also contains a nifty section of the most current hot topics called The Hottest Issues and Answers for CityVille that is the red heading on the left side of the CityVille help page. Click any of the links in this section to find answers to some of the most common issues affecting CityVille players at that moment.

Replacing lost items

Lost items are one of the most common CityVille problems requiring support from Zynga. The company has specific criteria for when and how lost items can be replaced:

- In general, Zynga replaces only *purchased* items that were lost because of an in-game error or glitch.

  As of this writing, Zynga doesn't restore *free* gifts lost because of in-game bugs.

  Zynga either replaces the purchase or refunds the purchase price in City Cash or City Coins.

- Neither purchased nor free items lost because of *user error* — such as accidentally deleting or selling an item, or sending a gift to the wrong person — will be replaced.

- Money will not be refunded for an accidental purchase of an item from the Build menu.

- If your Facebook account is compromised by another user, with or without your consent, Zynga doesn't replace any item that might have been lost or deleted as a result.

  Take necessary precautions to secure your account, as discussed earlier in this chapter.

You can read details about CityVille's full Item Restoration Policy by visiting

```
http://zynga.custhelp.com/app/answers/detail/a_id/3266
```

Web Resources

Even though this book is a handy reference for nearly everything you need to know about CityVille, the game changes. For the latest information on the latest happenings in and around CityVille, try the Web sites described in the following sections and the official CityVille forums discussed in detail in Chapter 2.

Games.com blog

```
http://blog.games.com/category/cityville
```

What's great about the CityVille section of the Games.com blog is that it provides an informational write-up in addition to screenshots of new game features. There are also helpful tips and walkthrough articles to teach you how to best utilize your time while in your city. The Games.com blog is typically updated every day, sometimes more than once a day. It also has an active readership, which usually means many comments on its posts. Games.com is also very active on Facebook (`www.facebook.com/gamescom`) and Twitter (`@gamesdotcom`), so if you don't get the chance to head directly over to its site (even though you should really, really try) you can keep up to date with what it's up to via social media.

CityVille Feed

```
www.cityvillefeed.com
```

One of the most comprehensive Web sites related to the game is CityVille Feed. CityVille Feed is updated several times per day with CityVille's lastest happenings, including new item releases and features, guides, tips, reviews, and general news. In addition to news, it has forums, a wiki, and an FAQ section to get you started with the game.

You can also follow CityVille Feed on Facebook, as shown in Figure 10-5.

```
www.facebook.com/cityvillefeed
```

Figure 10-5: The CityVille Feed Facebook Page.

CityVille Wiki

```
http://cityville.wikia.com/wiki/cityville_wiki
```

The content on CityVille Wiki is user-generated by those who love and excel at the game. This site is updated frequently, and new pages are being added all the time because Zynga constantly updates the game with fun, new f eatures!

CityVille Freak

```
http://cityvillefreaks.com
```

From the creators of the über-popular FarmVille Web site, Farmville Freak, comes CityVille Freak. Touted as the #1 Unofficial Fan Page, this site has a ton of information and even more images of upcoming features of the game. New information is added frequently, so be sure to bookmark this site and check back frequently. CityVille Freak also has a Facebook Page, as shown in Figure 10-6, that's worth liking.

Figure 10-6: The CityVille Freak Facebook Fan Page.

CityVille Freak has an active following, so there are lots of conversations going on via comments. Read through them, and something is bound to pique your interest.

Technical Matters: Troubleshooting and Game Enhancements

In This Chapter

▶ Taking a screenshot of your city

▶ Dealing with common CityVille bugs and glitches

As of this writing, CityVille is younger than a year old, and the developers at Zynga are constantly developing new features and updating content. Although this constant development means that you get to try new features as they're added to the game, it also means that the game may not be as stable as your average retail release. In fact, you can expect CityVille to be in Beta version for a while yet.

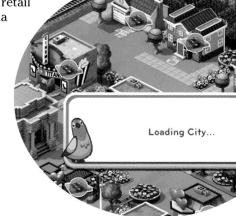

In this chapter, we tell you how to deal with some of the more common technical problems you may encounter while playing the game, and show you how to take advantage of some of the more technically advanced features in the game. The technical hiccups are a frustrating part of playing such a new Web-based game, but many times it just means that Zynga is doing its part in providing you with a very enjoyable gaming experience!

Taking a Picture of Your City

Although your neighbors can see your city at any time with a quick in-game visit, showing off your city to people who don't play the game can be a little tougher. To help with that, you can use your computer to capture a screenshot and save it as a digital image by following the steps in the next sections.

Getting ready to take a screenshot

Whether you're on a PC or a Mac, take these steps to prepare to capture an image of your screen:

1. **Turn on high-quality graphics by clicking the Eye icon in the upper-left corner of the Settings menu until the icon turns white.**

   Doing so ensures that your screenshot is of the best quality available.

2. **Click the Full Screen icon in the Settings menu.**

   The play area expands to take up your entire monitor, increasing the size of in-game details and how much you can see of your city.

3. **Arrange the scene to your liking to focus on the parts of your city you want to show.**

   See Chapter 3 for more on using the click + drag feature to position your city.

Taking a screenshot (Windows)

Here are the steps to capturing a shot of your city if you're on Windows:

1. **Press the Print Screen key on your keyboard.**

   You usually find this key near the Insert, Home, Delete, and End keys on the right side of the keyboard. Press Print Screen (it might be labeled Prt Sc, PrtScn, or some other variation) to save a copy of your current screen to the *Clipboard* (a temporary storage area).

2. **To get the image off the Clipboard, open Paint by choosing Start⇨ All Programs⇨Accessories and then locating the Paint program.**

   You can also open the Paint program by choosing typing Paint in the search box at the bottom of the Start menu. If you're comfortable using a different image-editing program, you can open it instead.

3. **Choose Edit⇨Paste.**

   A copy of the screen you captured in Step 1 is placed on the Paint (or other image-editing application's) canvas. You may need to click and drag the blue square in the lower-right corner to resize your picture and capture the entire captured screen. As a shortcut, you can also use the keyboard combination Ctrl+V to paste your image onto the canvas.

4. **Edit your picture as desired.**

   You may want to add text or cut off certain unsightly elements by using the Crop feature.

5. **Choose File⇨Save As.**

   The Save Picture dialog box appears.

6. **Enter a filename and select a location and file type for your image; then click Save.**

   Choose your file type wisely because some computers may not be able to open all the options you can save the image as. You can play it safe by choosing the most common file types: JPEG, GIF, or TIFF. The picture of your city is saved on your computer.

Certain file types, such as TIFF, save a higher-quality image than others. Although this is great for showing off your fantastic city in all its glory, this also means the file size is considerably larger. If you plan to e-mail this image, be sure to select a smaller file type, such as JPEG. The quality is still good, and the e-mail is less likely to get kicked back from an Internet service provider (ISP) for being too large for your recipient's mailbox.

Taking a screenshot (Mac)

Apple's Mac OS offers a few convenient keyboard shortcuts for taking shots of your city or any other elements on your screen:

- ✔ **To save the current screen,** press ⌘+Shift+3. Doing so saves the current screen to your desktop in a PNG file containing the words *Screen shot* and the date and time in the filename.

- ✔ **To save part of the screen:**

  1. *Press ⌘+Shift+4 to transform your cursor into a crosshair.*

  2. *Click and drag this crosshair to create a box around the area of the screen you want to capture.*

  3. *Release the mouse to save a PNG file of the captured section to your desktop.*

Troubleshooting Common Bugs and Glitches

Although CityVille is generally pretty stable, bugs and glitches can occasionally interrupt your game play, which can be very frustrating when all you really want to do is work on improving your city! These glitches can be anything from having trouble loading the game to losing actions you just performed and game items. This section outlines some of the most common problems you might encounter while playing CityVille as well as some simple ways to deal with them.

You can resolve many issues by reloading the CityVille Web page, restarting the Web browser, or restarting the computer. If other suggested fixes don't work, try those potential solutions in that order. Many issues are simply caused by temporary problems on Zynga's servers and may be resolved by the next time you load the game.

Attempting to connect to the server

When your game loses connection to Zynga's servers, the game reports that it's attempting to connect with the server, as shown in Figure 11-1. All this technical mumbo-jumbo simply means that Zynga's game servers are having trouble tracking and saving the current status of your city (which, as we describe in Chapter 2, is stored in the "cloud" of Zynga's servers). These errors can happen at any time, but performing a lot of tasks in a short period of time or placing large quantities of buildings or decorations too rapidly seems to cause these errors to appear more often. This error also contains the dreaded missing neighbors box, as discussed in the section "Neighbors' profile pictures" later in this chapter.

Figure 11-1: An Attempting to Connect to the Server error message.

You can wait out this one, but more often than not, the game will just end up refreshing itself. In the interest of saving some time, you may want to take the bull by the horns and refresh the game yourself. Any city actions you performed in the last few minutes may not appear after your city reloads, but don't worry — you can still perform those actions again.

If you continue working in your city without refreshing the browser after receiving this warning, all your hard work may be lost. That's why it's a good idea to refresh your city as soon as possible after the warning appears to avoid losing more work.

Facebook News Feed posting

In some cases, the game freezes when you attempt to share an item with friends through your Facebook News Feed, or the Facebook News Feed dialog box fails to appear.

This occasional problem has no known fix. Reloading your browser page allows you to continue playing, but you may no longer be able to share the item you were trying to post.

Your neighbors, not you, suffer most from this error.

Performance

Sometimes, game animation appears choppy or laggy, or the game takes longer than normal to respond to mouse clicks. Many times this happens when you visit a neighbor that has a very elaborate city. Here are a few possible solutions to try:

- ✔ Click the Eye icon in the lower-left corner of the Settings menu to reduce the graphic quality of the game.
- ✔ Close other programs or browser tabs that are open on your computer.
- ✔ Load CityVille in a different Web browser.

Loading

So it's time to play, when the game comes to a halt before you take a step. The game fails to load and freezes at 76 percent or 92 percent on the loading screen or after you're into your city. As if things couldn't get any worse, all your streets have magically disappeared, which causes your buildings to show a red circle with a line through them, signifying that they're not connected to roads, as shown in Figure 11-2. Alternatively, Adobe Flash Player may report that the plugin has crashed, as shown in Figure 11-3. Whew!

Figure 11-2: Where have all your streets gone?

Figure 11-3: An Adobe Flash Player plugin crash.

Have no fear; your streets haven't been taken from you. Try these options to get back on the road:

- **Close your browser completely and reload the page.** Often the game will go ahead and work on the second loading.

- **Clear the cache in your Web browser and reload your city.** Chapter 2 shows how to clear the cache in most popular browsers.

- **Install the latest version of Adobe's Flash Player, as detailed in Chapter 2.** You may need to uninstall your current Flash Player first.

This is one of the more common issues, and Zynga has been working hard to correct it. So hard, in fact, that in addition to the suggestions we provide here, Zynga took the time to write its own fix-its for this issue. To access these instructions, go to

```
http://zynga.custhelp.com/app/answers/detail/a_id/600
```

Renaming your city or business

So now you realize that naming your city *MyExIsAJerkVille* wasn't such a good idea, eh? Or maybe that naming your bridal shop *Don't Do It Bridal* was a little over the top?

If you've changed your mind about your city or business name, you're in luck — for the moment. As of this writing, you can e-mail Zynga tech support and request a name change by giving them the new name in the form of "I want to rename my city *XXX*" or "I want to rename my bridal shop *XXX*." As long as the name is 18 characters or fewer and isn't offensive or rude, the customer support team is happy to help.

Zynga may take away this ability at any time, so be sure to name wisely the first time around!

You accidently removed your franchise HQ

Oops! You accidently deleted the headquarters (HQ) of one of your franchise buildings. Or, your purposely deleted it in the hopes of gaining more space and then realized this may have been a really (really) bad idea. Will all your hard work building your burger joint empire disappear in one fell swoop?

Relax, your franchises are safe and sound. Believe it or not, you don't need to place a HQ in your city to maintain your franchises, as discussed in Chapter 6:

- The **good news** is that if you refresh your page, a new HQ shows up in your Inventory box.

- The **bad news** is that you have to rebuild it from the ground up after you place it. You can choose whether you want to place it, but keep in mind that your Inventory box can hold only up to 2,000 items. Although that may seem like a lot right now, you'd be surprised at how quickly space disappears — especially if you have a lot of friends sending you gifts or you're completing collections quickly.

An error occurred

This description of the error is helpful, huh?

```
An Error has Occurred
```

This message typically occurs when you attempt to help a neighbor or accept a gift from your neighbor via the Game Requests page.

If you get any errors while playing, this is probably the best one to get! Even though one would expect this error to mean the gift was lost or your offer for help was in vain, this is not the case. You still see the gift in your inventory, and your neighbor stills receive your help. See? We told you this was one of the good guys! There was nothing to worry about.

Neighbors' profile pictures

After your city loads, you're met with a thick white bar where your beloved neighbors once resided, as shown in Figure 11-4. This error sometimes works in conjunction with one of the other connection errors.

Figure 11-4: Missing neighbors.

Here are a few options to try when this happens:

- ✔ Refresh the page.
- ✔ Clear your cache.

If the issue persists, Zynga's servers might be acting up. Try coming back later to see whether the issue is resolved.

Experiencing technical difficulties

The Technical Difficulties error is pretty much a catch-all. Most of the time it just means that there is an issue with Zynga's servers, and the good people at Zynga are no doubt diligently working on it to correct the problem. As you can see from Figure 11-5, this error is sometimes accompanied by missing pictures on your neighbors' profiles.

Figure 11-5: They seem to be experiencing some technical difficulties.

As the error message box helpfully instructs you, click the Okay button to refresh the page. If you find that the page is frozen, as sometimes happens if you are in full-screen mode, try refreshing your Web browser.

Saving

If your status isn't saved correctly at the end of a session, tasks performed during the last play session aren't reflected when you load the game the next time.

Problems with saving most commonly occur right after users expand their land and rearrange their cities to accommodate their new space.

In addition to sometimes nullifying hours of work, in extreme cases, these saving issues can cause you to lose in-game currency with nothing to show for it, or to lose accumulated Energy.

Zynga recommends staying on your city for at least 15 minutes before closing your Web browser or leaving the CityVille page to avoid problems with saving your actions. If you need to leave the CityVille page for any reason, Zynga recommends clicking the Facebook logo to return to your Facebook home page before moving on to other Web pages.

If a saving issue causes you to lose any in-game currency or Energy, contact Zynga support using the methods detailed in Chapter 10.

If a pop-up message tells you that your city is saving and `Please do not close your browser`, take it seriously. Please don't close your browser!

Full-screen mode is not working

Clicking the Full Screen button doesn't cause the game to enter full-screen mode as it should.

Sorry, but there isn't a solution at this time. In the meantime, you can try one of these general fixes:

- Refresh the page.
- Clear your cache. (See Chapter 2.)
- Close CityVille and return to the game later.
- Close other programs or browser tabs that are open on your computer.
- Load CityVille in a different Web browser.

Running out of Energy

Running out of Energy may not be an error message per se, but it's a message box, as shown in Figure 11-6, that appears frequently, so we think it's worth a mention.

Sometimes you're so engrossed in your game play that you don't pay attention to the important little meter at the top of your screen. Because of this, you might be performing more tasks, such as collecting from houses, that although important, take up Energy instead of ones, such as collecting from your stores, that could net you more Coins. For more information on being efficient in your city, see Chapter 9.

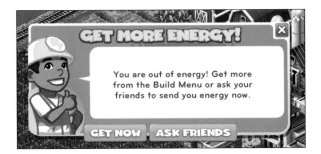

Figure 11-6: Keep your Energy level high so you don't get this message.

A few tips can keep you playing:

✔ Pay attention to the amount of Energy you have stored up:

   • When you start your game play, it's a good idea to start it with a full Energy meter, which you can get by helping neighbors, purchasing it from the Build menu, or just waiting the five minutes for it to be restored.

   • Perform more important tasks first while leaving others.

✔ Put out a call for Energy gifts before you run out to give your neighbors time to see the message and (hopefully) respond by sending you some Batteries to keep your meter full.

For more information on using your Energy resources wisely, see Chapter 7.

The CityVille Has Been Enhanced Notification

One of the most exciting pop-up notifications in all of CityVille is the CityVille Has Been Enhanced message, as shown in Figure 11-7. This means that Zynga has just released a new version of CityVille with new features or game play fixes. When you see this notification, click the Okay button to reload your city.

Figure 11-7: The CityVille Has Been Enhanced notification.

Often, when your city reloads, additional pop-up notifications let you know that new features are now available for your city. This new content often includes new goals or items added to the Build menu. If no new pop-up notifications appear when your city reloads, the new updates probably applied primarily to behind-the-scenes fixes, including improvements to the game's stability and security.

Check the Build menu to see whether any new items are available, just in case.

Losing your connection

The game loses its connection to Zynga's game servers for any of a variety of reasons, and when it does, you see the Lost Connection error message, as shown in Figure 11-8. Many times it's just a hiccup with Zynga's servers that corrects itself with a refresh of the page.

Figure 11-8: Oops! The connection was lost.

Try these options to refresh the game and reestablish a connection to the server:

- Click the Okay button in the message box to refresh the page.
- Refresh your Internet browser.

Part IV
The Part of Tens

*T*he final part of this book consists of a series of lists containing ten juicy topics that make playing CityVille fun.

Read about ten "go-to" items that make City life a little bit sweeter in Chapter 12.

Chapter 13 lists our ten common City types — see where you fit into the bunch.

Finally in Chapter 14 we spill some secrets on what a few of CityVille's most successful Mayors did to get to where they are today.

Ten Go-To Items

*W*ith dozens of items available through the CityVille Build menu (as we detail in Chapter 4), it can sometimes be hard to decide which one is right for you. That only applies, though, if you choose an item that's not listed in this chapter.

Every item in this list has been picked because it's the best in its class in some way. Not all these items are available from the very start of the game, and some might be outside your current price range, but keep playing and saving and soon you'll be coming back for these items again and again.

Sushi Bar

- **Type:** Business
- **Requirements:** 2,300 population
- **Cost:** 12,500 Coins
- **Footprint:** 3 x 3
- **Supply with:** 110 Goods
- **Collect earnings for:** 605 Coins

Do what you can to work your way up to that 2,300 population threshold as quickly as you can because after you do, you unlock the money-earning Sushi Bar powerhouse. Each Good you invest into a Sushi Bar comes back as a whopping 5.5 Coins when you collect your earnings — the best such ratio in the game. Not only that, but the relatively modest 12,500 Coin cost is paid back after you collect from the Sushi Bar just over 20 times. After that, the Sushi Bar is a powerhouse of pure profit forevermore.

The Sushi Bar does have some failings compared to other high-earning buildings, though these drawbacks mostly become apparent further down the road. Although the Sushi Bar pays for itself much faster than the Cinema, for instance, the subsequent long-term profits lag well behind after a while — especially if the Cinema is bolstered by some good decorations. The Sushi Bar's small 3-x-3 footprint also makes it slightly harder to pump with decoration bonuses, as well (see Chapter 9).

Still, the Sushi Bar is a great choice as a business that builds up your nest egg quickly without setting you back for too long.

Cinema

- ✔ **Type:** Business
- ✔ **Requirements:** Complete the Cinema Investment quest
- ✔ **Cost:** 100,000 Coins
- ✔ **Footprint:** 4 x 4
- ✔ **Supply with:** 140 Goods
- ✔ **Collect earnings for:** 749 Coins

First the bad news: That 100,000 Coin cost means you need to collect from an undecorated Cinema over 130 times before you make back your initial investment. And even though you have to shell out a hefty 140 Goods every time you want to supply your Cinema, smaller businesses, such as the Sushi Bar and Wedding Store, can return more Coins per Good. Then there's the oversized 4-x-4 footprint, which can make the Cinema stick out like a sore thumb in your careful grid.

But the Cinema's upsides help make up for these problems. The biggest of these upsides is the massive 749 Coin return for each collection, which easily outclasses all cheaper businesses. This strong base-earnings level makes each decoration attached to a Cinema that much more meaningful — in fact, a well-decorated Cinema can easily return thousands of Coins every time you collect from it. Not only that, but the Cinema's 4-x-4 size means it can potentially host more decorations than a smaller business (see Chapter 9).

But the best thing about the Cinema might be the way you unlock it by completing a quest, rather than by satisfying some stringent level or population requirements. This means a diligent player can unlock the Cinema well before many other high-earning businesses. As a window into the world of truly lucrative businesses, the Cinema can't be beat.

Tower Eats

- **Type:** Business
- **Requirements:** None
- **Cost:** 1,000,000 Coins
- **Footprint:** 4 x 4
- **Supply with:** 165 Goods
- **Collect earnings for:** 900 Coins

With a cost of a cool million Coins and basic statistics that don't seem that much better than much cheaper businesses, Tower Eats may at first seem like a sucker bet. But don't be so sure. With a 900 Coin return per collection, Tower Eats is both the Coins you can receive for a single click (without the aid of decorations, that is) and the best conversion of Goods into Coins in the game. And that's before you place a ton of decorations around your Tower Eats to send that number well into the thousands.

True, even at thousands of Coins per click, it takes a while to pay back that massive million Coin investment. But remember, you're in this for the long haul. After that initial investment is finally paid off, your highly decorated Tower Eats will become by far the best profit-generating machine in your city, bar none. At that point, you'll wonder how you got by with the paltry Coin returns you got from lesser businesses.

Rocky Hill

- **Type:** Decoration
- **Requirements:** 15 neighbors
- **Cost:** 24,000 Coins
- **Footprint:** 4 x 4
- **Bonus:** 20-percent payout

Most of the decorations in CityVille are utterly interchangeable. Sure, you might prefer the look of Blue Flowers to that of the Shade Tree. Or maybe you're more into the granite permanence of the Barricade or Bronze Statue. In any case, the small differences in cost belie the fact that all these decorations, as well as most others, provide just a 1-percent bonus for each square of land they take up.

And then there's the Rocky Hill. True, the initial investment of 24,000 Coins can seem a little steep at first, and the 4-x-4 footprint makes it hard to place in the nooks and crannies in your city. But that large footprint comes with an even larger 20-percent payout bonus, a good 4-percent higher than most of the smaller decorations you could put in the equivalent space.

Not only that, but the Rocky Hill's expanded size comes with an expanded area of effect compared with smaller decorations. This means that, with careful placement (see Chapter 9), your Rocky Hill can touch significantly more businesses than that dinky Flower Pot or Shade Tree. With careful placement and a few strong businesses around, that 24,000 Coin cost will be paid off before you know it.

Tennis Court

- **Type:** Decoration
- **Requirements:** None
- **Cost:** 35 Cash
- **Footprint:** 8 x 4
- **Bonus:** 64-percent payout

If you're looking for pure payout-boosting power, you can't do better than this decoration. In fact, you can't even come close — the decorations that come closest to equaling the mighty Tennis Court only provide a 32-percent bonus to surrounding businesses and homes. Not only that, but the Tennis Court provides this massive bonus while taking up only 32 squares of city space, making it among the most efficient bonus decorations in the game for its size.

There is a downside, of course, and that comes in the form of the massive 35 City Cash cost. Earning that much Cash requires saving for dozens of levels, completing promotional offers from CityVille partners, or breaking out your real wallet to get some virtual scratch. And, of course, the court's awkward 8-x-4 size requires clearing a large space to place it. Still, if you can afford the Cash and the space, there are few better items to invest in.

Carousel

- **Type:** Decoration
- **Requirements:** Complete Animal Farm quest
- **Cost:** 25,000 Coins
- **Footprint:** 3 x 3
- **Population limit increase:** 700

Some CityVille players see community buildings as nothing more than a necessary evil — a waste of space that's unfortunately needed to increase that important population limit. Those players are somewhat right, but if you have to add a Community Building, you could do a lot worse than the Carousel. For a mere 25,000 Coins — a mid-range cost as far as community buildings are concerned — you get a whopping 700-member increase in your population limit, making for one of the better population-increase-to-Coin ratios in the game.

The hidden strength of the Carousel, though, comes in its tiny 3-x-3 footprint. Not only does this make the Carousel the smallest Community Building in the game by a good nine squares, but it also makes it the most efficient population increaser for its size until the Courthouse, which you can't unlock until Level 55. This mix of small size and small cost with a relatively big population increase make this one of the least evil of these necessary evils.

Peas

> ✔ **Type:** Crop
> ✔ **Requirements:** Reach Level 25
> ✔ **Cost:** 85 Coins per plot
> ✔ **Harvest for:** 155 Goods
> ✔ **Harvest time:** 3.1 days

We know what you're thinking: "Over *three days* before I can collect my Goods? But my businesses need supplying *now!* Who can afford to wait that long?" A better question might be who can afford *not* to wait that long. At over 1.8 Goods per invested Coin, peas are one of the most cost-efficient crops in the game.

But their real efficiency is measured not in Coins, but in Energy. Face it: There are better things you could be doing with your Energy than spending it harvesting crops. By giving you an impressive 155 Goods per harvesting click, peas conserve that precious Energy for those better uses.

There's a beneficial side to that long ripening time: It takes over six days for ripe peas to wither, giving you plenty of time to accumulate the Energy you need to collect entire vast fields of the stuff.

Eggplant

- ✔ **Type:** Crop
- ✔ **Requirements:** Reach Level 6
- ✔ **Cost:** 28 Coins per plot
- ✔ **Harvest for:** 30 Goods
- ✔ **Harvest time:** 1 hour

Sometimes you just don't have the crop space or the time necessary to wait for a pea crop to ripen. In these cases, a lot of farmers look to five-minute strawberries for a quick burst of Goods.

But strawberries are a sucker bet, in the long run. Although strawberries generate Goods extremely quickly, they also require a *lot* of Energy to harvest for a small amount of Goods. Unless you have a whole lot of Energy Batteries handy, 15 Goods per Energy just isn't going to cut it for most purposes.

Eggplant provides a good compromise on this score. This crop generates 30 Goods an hour, which is 6 times worse than strawberries. But that slowness actually gives you a chance to regain enough Energy to actually harvest all those Goods without too much Energy pain. Plant a field of 12 eggplants when your Energy is empty, and an hour later you'll have a field with 360 Goods *and* the Energy to harvest it. Sure, you'll pay a premium for this quick access to Goods, but if you weren't in a hurry, you'd be planting peas, right?

Boats

- ✔ **Type:** Shipping
- ✔ **Requirements:** Pier
- ✔ **Cost:** 100 Coins
- ✔ **Footprint:** 2 x 3

The best way to think of boats is as a super-efficient farm plot. Both the boat and the plot cost 100 Coins, but the boat is clearly superior in its good production abilities:

- ✔ Every crop you can plant on your farm has an equivalent shipping mission that takes the same amount of time, yet generates more Goods.

- ✔ Shipping missions generate those Goods with a smaller outlay of Coins and Energy than the similar crops.

The catch? Well, you have to build a pier before you can buy a boat, and that means expanding your city out to some generally less-than-useful coastal areas. Each pier can maintain only eight boats, as well, which adds a hidden cost of thousands of Coins if you want to expand your shipping capacity.

Trust us, though, you'll be thanking us for this recommendation when the Goods come rolling in faster than ever through those shipping missions.

Expansions

- ✔ **Type:** Expansion
- ✔ **Requirements:** Level 15 and 300 neighbors for first expansion (increases with each subsequent expansion; see Chapter 4)
- ✔ **Cost:** 20,000 Coins and one zoning permit for first expansion (increases with each subsequent expansion; see Chapter 4)
- ✔ **Footprint:** 12-x-12 blocks of additional usable land

After playing CityVille for a while, it quickly becomes clear that land space is one of the biggest limiting factors in the game. Because every building and decoration takes up a little bit of this precious resource, think of expansions as the item that makes all the other items possible. If you have the means, these should almost always be one of the first things you look at buying.

Of course, getting those means is the tricky part. Each 12-x-12 block expansion requires one more zoning permit than the previous one, as well as more Coins and population than you needed to expand before. (See Chapter 4.) Although the price can get pretty hefty, the benefit of having more space to place everything else you need is nearly immeasurable. Whatever they're asking, pay it.

Ten Common City Types

*O*ne of the great things about CityVille is the relative freedom it offers players to design a city to their liking. With dozens of available buildings and decorations and the ability to expand your city space in all directions, practically an infinite number of different city configurations are available. This means that no two CityVille cities are likely to be exactly alike.

That doesn't mean there won't be some similarities between cities, though. In visiting your neighbors' cities, you're likely to stumble across many, if not most, of the basic types we list in this chapter. We explain each common city type, as we've identified it, and give you some pointers for how to react when you see it in a neighboring city. We even point out some helpful tips you can figure out through careful observation of that particular city type. Don't you feel smarter already?

The Farm

Vast, wide fields full of all sorts of crops dominate this common city type. Whether out of habit learned through excessive play of fellow Facebook game FarmVille or out of some inner desire for a more pastoral landscape, the owner of this city has caused it to tilt from the usual urban look to a much more rural tone.

Which isn't a bad idea, actually — crops and the Goods they provide are key to powering the businesses that can earn the most in-game Coins as quickly as possible. Having more farmland also give you the space and freedom to plant highly efficient, slow-to-ripen crops, such as peas, without worrying about long, Goods-free dry spells.

When visiting a farm, tending to your neighbors' crops is a no-brainer. That means watering and harvesting; the latter of which provides precious Goods for your own use as well.

The Overdecorated

Productive, profitable buildings are just a distracting nuisance for the owner of this type of city. Where some see their CityVille city as a place to build a bustling city full of people and businesses, the overdecorated city owner sees a blank canvas, on which to paint as many gaudy, highly animated decorations as possible.

In an overdecorated city, the actual tangible earning benefits of the decorations are almost beside the point. Variety and clever arrangement are the name of the game here, with multicolored flowers, Stop Signs, and Picnic Tables often precisely aligned to make eye-catching mosaics. In fact, an overdecorated city is one of the only places you're likely to see those rare decorations that don't actually provide percentage bonuses to nearby businesses.

Owners of overdecorated cities need a lot of Coins to keep their decorating habits going strong, so help them by sending tour buses to any businesses they happen to have. If you can, try sending those buses to businesses that are surrounded by a particularly dense and lucrative array of decorations. Maybe your neighbor will get the hint that their decorations are useful for more than just looking pretty . . . .

The Packed

Most CityVille cities have a bit of empty space, either out of economic necessity or aesthetic prerogative. Not the packed city. Every available inch of space in this type of city is loaded with some sort of building or decoration, to the point where some buildings and decorations can be completely hidden behind others in the game's isometric view.

Packed cities are primarily filled with the largest, most ostentatious buildings available, with the occasional nook or cranny filled by a small decoration. Packed city owners are always desperate for more space to pack with more stuff, so be sure to send them zoning permits as often as possible to help their efforts along.

The Sprawling

The packed city's opposite number, a sprawling city, is blessed (or plagued) with a surfeit of space. Possibly inspired by the suburbs that have come to dominate wide swaths of the United States, the sprawling city owner has invested huge sums of money and zoning permits into as many expansions as he could, and has yet to spend the resources or the effort to buy the buildings and decorations needed to fill all that space.

Sprawling cities are identified by dozens of citizens wandering long, empty roads to get from their houses to the few businesses dotting the landscape. You can also identify them by the huge, unbroken gaps in the scenery. Sprawling city owners seem to enjoy the Winter Cover decoration because the soothing white snow cover makes these empty patches look somehow more appealing than a normal, grassy green.

You can encourage these city owners and their wasteful sprawl by sending more zoning permits, but we recommend sending as many decorations as possible instead. Who knows, maybe the owner will actually place some of these decorations in some of that open space, instead of letting them languish in her inventory. If you're really lucky, maybe she'll get the idea and turn her once sprawling city into an overdecorated city, instead! Will wonders never cease?

The Ultra-Efficient

No fuss, no muss, and no wasted space are the defining characteristics of this increasingly common city type. Every available square of this city is tuned to a highly specific purpose, to get the most Coins in the least time, with as little Energy as possible.

In general, ultra-efficient cities have a minimum of high-density housing and community buildings set aside in one neglected corner, possibly with huge swathes of farmland nearby to provide an endless stack of Goods. These are put into the service of a set of a few of the higher-earning businesses — such as Cinemas or Tower Eats — which are in turn surrounded by highly effective decorations to turbocharge their earning potential. Sidewalks and especially roads are at a bare minimum in these cities, as are the more beautiful but less functional decorations that dot many other cities.

Ultra-efficient city owners don't need any decorations as gifts, but they're always in need of Energy to help harvest their crops and collect from their few businesses. They're also probably on the lookout for zoning permits that give even more space that can be put toward their highly focused growth plans.

The Abandoned

Unfortunately, the tens of millions of people who have signed up to play CityVille include many millions who have given up on the game after a time. Maybe the real world has intruded on their gaming time. Maybe they got frustrated because not enough neighbors joined them in playing. Maybe they just grew bored with the game. In any case, their static cities can be a bit of a blight during your daily visits.

Having an abandoned city as a neighbor isn't all bad, though. Because nothing changes, you always know what to expect from this type of city. Plus, if your neighbor was thoughtful enough to plant some strawberries just before his departure, you can be sure these never-wither crops will always be available for harvest on your visit, netting you some much-needed Goods. Plus, a neighbor who's abandoned the game is one you don't have to waste time lavishing gifts on, so look on the bright side!

The Businesslike

Somehow, the owner of this city got the crazy idea that more is better when it comes to CityVille businesses. Unlike the few high-earning businesses of the ultra-efficient city, the businesslike city is more likely to be filled with lots of low-cost, low-earning businesses, lining every available street front location in a veritable shopper's paradise.

The only problem with a businesslike city, from the owner's perspective, is the vast amount of Energy it takes to collect from all those businesses — often for very little relative reward. Towns like this provide a cautionary tale of what can happen to your city if you're not willing to raze old, inefficient businesses and replace them with better buildings when you can afford to. Perhaps the businesslike city owner just can't be bothered to get rid of those sentimental first purchases.

In any case, there's not much to be done as a neighbor to help this city owner or convince him to change his ways. Perhaps a Facebook message is in order, recommending the purchase of this book to show him just how much more efficient his city could be . . . .

The Overpopulated

What businesses are to the businesslike city, housing and community buildings are to the overpopulated city. Endless rows of high-density housing like Brownstone Apartments line this city, usually punctuated by a tiny area packed to the gills with all the community buildings necessary to maintain a city that size.

On the plus side, an overpopulated city doesn't really need very many crops because there aren't very many businesses that need to be supplied with Goods (we sometimes wonder how the residents don't starve). On the downside, because housing units provide money much more slowly than businesses, overpopulated cities are usually light on the resources needed for quick expansion.

Not that that's necessarily a bad thing. Some players enjoy the slower pace and simple, more straightforward maintenance of a city filled with people instead of businesses. Help these fellow players by sending the Energy Batteries they need to collect all those piddling rents.

The Disorganized

Not every CityVille player has some larger plan in mind when placing buildings and decorations in their city. In fact, thanks to the way that new items slowly unlock in the Build menu (see Chapter 4), most CityVille cities end up as a disorganized mess with businesses, community buildings, and housing of all shapes and sizes sitting next to others without any thematic or functional purpose to the arrangement.

There's nothing wrong with keeping your city like this, really. You can have a perfectly functional city with buildings arranged all pell-mell. But getting your city organized logically can be helpful for one important reason — decorations. By placing your high-value businesses together, in a location next to a highly decorated area, you can really squeeze every drop of profit out of your Goods investment. Arranging these buildings and decorations randomly is like leaving in-game money on the table.

Plus, keeping like businesses and housing grouped together makes it simple to find what you're looking for when collection time comes around. Wouldn't it be nice not to have to hunt and scroll through your city just to find that one lonely coffee shop in the residential development? Remember, the Move tool can help a disorganized city become highly organized relatively easily.

The Balanced

The perfect city has just the right amount of housing, crops, businesses, community buildings, and decorations with everything placed in a way that's both aesthetically pleasing and relatively efficient. The balanced city makes money, but isn't so obsessed with money that the entire city becomes a sterile, lifeless cash machine. The balanced city is arranged in a visually pleasing manner, but not so much so that it ignores arrangements that could easily make more money.

In the end, the exact level of balance between all these competing concerns is really up to you. There's no one right way or wrong way to make your CityVille city. Like a dollhouse, part of the fun in CityVille is in arranging things just so and playing around with different setups until you find the one you like.

You can always destroy buildings and decorations that you feel just aren't working, and move ones that are in inconvenient locations to change your city's feel.

It's your city — build it how you want to.

Ten Habits of Highly Effective Mayors

*T*hroughout this book, we lay out dozens of bits of advice for effectively managing your CityVille city. But not everyone has the time or inclination to pore through hundreds of pages just for these tidbits. Consider this chapter a *Cliff's Notes* version of the rest of the book, where we lay out the ten most important things to remember when managing your city.

Maximize Your Energy Use

More than any other in-game resource, Energy is the one that most limits your growth potential in CityVille. If there were some code to unlock infinite Energy, it'd be trivial to just sit at the computer all day and quickly rack up practically infinite money from crops and businesses. Because there is no such code, however, maximizing your profits means maximizing the amount of Energy you have access to.

The simplest way to maximize your Energy use, as silly as it seems, is to just play the game frequently. Remember, when your Energy meter is full, you no longer earn free, bonus Energy every five minutes. This wasted time, essentially becomes wasted Energy when you come back to the game with a meter no more full than it was hours ago.

Consider a player whose Energy meter can contain the current maximum of 30 Energy. If that player checks in to the game every 2.5 hours and uses all 30 Energy each time, he's burning through nearly 300 Energy every day. Compared to the player who just checks in once a day, the regular checker is getting nearly ten times as many useful actions over the same period of time.

Of course, being this efficient with your Energy means forgoing things like sleeping and leaving the house once in a while, which we don't recommend. Still, there's likely a happy medium you can find where you check in and burn some Energy a few times each day, thus unlocking the Energy-earning power of your time away. When you have a little more time available, don't forget to visit neighbors to squeeze out few more Energy, as well.

Prioritize Your Actions

After playing CityVille for a while, you quickly get to the point where your limited Energy isn't enough to complete everything you want to do during a single play session. You just have too many crop lots to harvest, too many businesses to collect from, too many new buildings to build, and so on. When this happens, prioritize what potential actions are the most important — and most lucrative — use of your limited Energy.

Clearly, not all clicks are created equal in this situation. Follow this order:

1. If you have crops that are about to wither, these take precedence over everything else so you don't lose your expensive farming investment for good.

2. After farming, collecting from businesses is usually your best bet for earning a lot of Coins with just a few Energy.

   Make sure to click your most profitable and decorated businesses before wasting Energy on others.

3. Check in on your community buildings, which can provide free Energy and lots of bonus Coins through the Bonus bar (see Chapter 7).

4. If you have leftover Energy, consider building some new buildings or clearing trees from recent expansions.

You don't have to use all of your Energy every time you check in to the game. You can always save that extra Energy for later, allowing you to check in to a full Energy meter that much sooner. In other words, don't click a dinky little Country Home just because you don't have anything better to do at the moment because you may well have something better to do later.

Support Your Neighbors

Playing CityVille really gives new meaning to the phrase "doing well by doing good." Helping your neighboring cities might seem like a purely altruistic act at first — saving your neighbor Energy and providing them with additional Coins and Goods. Being a good Samaritan in this way can make you feel all warm and squishy, but the personal benefits go well past that.

Every time you visit a neighbor, you get bonuses in the form of Coins, Goods and, most importantly, Energy, just for showing up. Not only that, but you get five bonus Energy to use in the neighbor's city, earning you further Coins or Goods as you help.

These neighbor visits don't cost you anything but time, and the resources you get from them can be invaluable in giving you a leg up over the competition. In fact, if you're not visiting your neighbors as much as possible, you're essentially leaving free resources on the table.

Furthermore, visiting your neighboring cities is a great way to get inspiration and ideas for new arrangements and building mixes for your own city. Why count on your own imagination when you can steal — er, we mean *borrow* — ideas from your neighbors at no additional cost?

Sure, going through all the motions of dozens of neighbor visits can take awhile, but hey, Rome wasn't built in a day.

Destroy Old Buildings

We know that it can be tough to tear down that first little Suburban House you set up in your CityVille city many moons ago. There are so many memories associated with it, after all. The first time you got the keys. The first time you brought the baby home. The little tick marks on the doorjamb showing little Jimmy's growth over the year . . . .

What's that? You're saying none of that stuff happens in a virtual CityVille house? Hey, you're right! So there's no need to be sentimental with old buildings that have outlived their usefulness. After the virtual money starts rolling in — and better buildings start getting unlocked — clear out the space taken up by less efficient buildings and fill it with some that have a little more earning power.

True, selling a building and paying what can be a substantial sum of Coins to replace it isn't great for the short-term bottom line. But smart players think about the long term and how much more money a newer, more profitable building can make over weeks, months, and years of steady collections. Remember, city space is one of the most precious resources you have, and wasting it with anything less than the best building you can is like throwing money out the window.

Use the Bonus Bar

One of the great things about CityVille is that it doesn't require quick reflexes or frenetic clicking to play; you can do everything at your own pace. But for those who are willing to focus a little bit, there are huge cash bonuses to be had by collecting resource icons as quickly as possible in an unbroken chain.

As we outline in Chapter 7, the Bonus bar can be the source of literally thousands of extra Coins every time you check in with the game. To make sure you're getting the maximum bonus, make sure you've completely filled up your Energy meter before you start clicking, and that you have a good number of buildings and crops to collect from.

After you start collecting those Resource icons, don't forget to continue clicking buildings and crops to keep new icons coming. Alternating between clicking resource icons and buildings and crops is a good way to make sure you don't hit a gap that might let the Bonus bar falter.

Focus your clicking on one small area of the city, if possible, so you don't waste time scrolling between disparate areas. And don't forget to collect from your community buildings, which provide tons of icons with each click, plus some bonus Energy to keep the streak going even longer.

Focus on the Long Term

Pop quiz, hot shot. One business costs a mere 12,500 Coins to purchase and provides 600 or so Coins every time you collect from it. Another costs a cool million Coins to purchase, but provides 900 Coins every time you collect from it. Which one is the better buy?

If you said the first one (the Sushi Bar), you may be too short-sighted to have what it really takes to maintain a truly profitable city. Sure, you'll pay off that Sushi Bar pretty quickly and make a decent enough profit off of it well after that. Project long enough into the future, though, and the profitability from the million Coin Tower Eats investment will eventually outpace the cheaper investment, especially if you augment them both with lucrative decorations.

CityVille isn't a standard type of game with a finish line and a Game Over screen. It's designed to be played regularly for weeks, months, even years — as long as you stay interested, really. Over that time scale, trading a big investment now for bigger regular returns well into the future is a shrewd business decision, and one that will pay off over time.

Decorate Effectively

A lot of city owners pack their cities with as many businesses as they can, cramming every inch of available space with some profit-generating enterprise or another. At first glance, this seems like a smart move — businesses are generally the most profitable use of land in the game. But those business-happy city managers would do well to rethink their position and replace a few of their businesses with some strategically placed decorations.

True, those decorations don't generate any profits themselves, but they make every nearby business that much more productive. This increased productivity can help make up for the initial cost of the decoration quite quickly, making each decoration practically a free money-making machine.

Although the businesses near a decoration will all generate more money, they don't require any additional Goods or Energy when compared to a non-decorated business, making that business much more efficient. Which would you rather do: Spend 2 Energy and 300 Goods collecting from 2 businesses, or spend 1 Energy and 150 Goods collecting the same money from 1 business with a 100-percent decoration bonus?

Not all decorations are created equal. Although most decorations provide only a 1-percent productivity boost for each square they occupy, some, such as the Rocky Hill and Expo Tent, are much more efficient for their footprint. These decorations might cost a lot at first, but with the right business nearby, the high cost can quickly come back in the form of extra collection money.

Expand for Your Life

Of all the limited resources in CityVille, city space is one of the most limited. Although you can earn more Energy just by waiting and you can earn more Coins and Cash just by playing the game, earning more space requires an actual in-game purchase. The first such expansion is relatively cheap, but each subsequent expansion costs more Coins and requires a larger population and more hard-to-get zoning permits from neighbors.

Without the extra space granted by constant expansion, your city will soon be a crowded, unmanageable mess. With extra space, however, your wildest city-building dreams can be yours for the taking. It might not seem as urgent as that new harvest of peas, but trust us when we tell you to make expansion a priority.

Check Your Facebook Feed

Chances are if you have a Facebook account, you already check your Wall and your notifications regularly. If not, you should definitely start if you want to succeed in CityVille.

If you've racked up a good number of neighbors, your News Feed is soon be filled with news from their cities, announcing everything from a new building to a new level reached. These news posts can be interesting in and of themselves, but the bonus links are the real attraction here, providing free Coins, Goods, and Experience Points for a click.

But the most lucrative part of the News Feed actually comes via requests from neighbors asking for one item or another. How so? Every time you send a gift using one of these links, you immediately get a copy of the same item added to your inventory as a thank you. Just like in life, it pays to be nice in CityVille. In CityVille though, the reward for being nice is a bit more immediate.

Buy as Much City You Can Afford

See those Coins sitting in your account? They're not doing anyone any good just sitting there, waiting to be spent. In CityVille, as in real life, the only way to make money is by spending money.

This doesn't mean you can't save up for things, of course. If you've really got your eye on Tower Eats, you can afford to be frugal for a bit and really work toward those million Coins. Of course, you might reach that million-Coin level faster if you spend some of your nest egg on more businesses that speed up your profit-making ability.

Striking the right balance between saving and spending can be tricky, but the one thing you definitely don't want to do is sit around with millions of Coins in your account. That kind of hoarding might fulfill a deep psychological need, but it's useless from a game play perspective. Money was meant to be spent so that's what you should do!

Index

● *G* ●